MAXnotes®

George Eliot's

Middlemarch

Text by
Gail Rae Rosensfit
(M.A., Hunter College)
Department of English
McKee Vocational Technical High School
Staten Island, New York

Illustrations by
Arnold Turovskiy

Research & Education Association

What MAXnotes® Will Do for You

This book is intended to help you absorb the essential contents and features of George Eliot's *Middlemarch* and to help you gain a thorough understanding of the work. The book has been designed to do this more quickly and effectively than any other study guide.

For best results, this **MAXnotes** book should be used as a companion to the actual work, not instead of it. The interaction between the two will greatly benefit you.

To help you in your studies, this book presents the most up-to-date interpretations of every section of the actual work, followed by questions and fully explained answers that will enable you to analyze the material critically. The questions also will help you to test your understanding of the work and will prepare you for discussions and exams.

Meaningful illustrations are included to further enhance your understanding and enjoyment of the literary work. The illustrations are designed to place you into the mood and spirit of the work's settings.

The **MAXnotes** also include summaries, character lists, explanations of plot, and section-by-section analyses. A biography of the author and discussion of the work's historical context will help you put this literary piece into the proper perspective of what is taking place.

The use of this study guide will save you the hours of preparation time that would ordinarily be required to arrive at a complete grasp of this work of literature. You will be well prepared for classroom discussions, homework, and exams. The guidelines that are included for writing papers and reports on various topics will prepare you for any added work which may be assigned.

The **MAXnotes** will take your grades "to the max."

Dr. Max Fogiel
Program Director

Contents

**Each Book includes List of Characters,
Summary, Analysis, Study Questions and
Answers, and Suggested Essay Topics.**

Introduction

The Life and Work of George Eliot

George Eliot was born Mary Ann Evans in Warwickshire, England, on November 22, 1819, to Robert Evans, Sr., a carpenter turned estate manager, and his second wife, the former Christiana Pearson. Ms. Evans' living siblings were an older half-brother and sister, Robert and Fanny, from her father's first marriage. She also had another older sister and brother, Christinia and Isaac, from the union between her father and mother. Politics, religion, and education were very important to the young Polly, as she was nicknamed. Her schooling began at age four, with a series of boarding schools, which her older siblings attended. Each school was more academically oriented than the last, which was pleasing to the intellectual and unattractive young girl. Her schooling temporarily ended when her mother died of breast cancer. She was brought home to keep house for her father because one of her sisters was already married and the other planned to marry within the year. Ms. Evans was 16 at this time.

Her father allowed her to order any books she chose. When she was 20, Signor Joseph Brezzi was hired to tutor her in German and then Italian. Although she was not at school, with friends such as Harriet Beecher Stowe, the publisher John Blackwood, and Mme. Eugene Bodichon (a champion of unpopular causes), her education continued. In the summer of 1841, after she moved with her father to Coventry, she studied astronomy and geology. She became a Freethinker, which prompted her father to ask her to leave his house. She was also very involved in women's issues and did not see the need for marriage. She had affairs with her neighbor, Charles Bray, despite her friendship with his wife, Cara, and with John Chapman, although she lived in his boarding house along with his wife and mistress. She and her father reconciled, provided that she make a token appearance in church periodically to save the family's reputation. She nursed him for the rest of his life, at the same time studying whatever interested her.

Upon his death, she called herself "Marian" and moved to London. She lived on her small inheritances from her father and aunt and her wages as the (secret) editor for Chapman's *Westminster Review*. This show of independence caused a further breach in the family. She fell in unrequited love with the confirmed bachelor editor of *The Economist*, Herbert Spencer, in 1852.

Fairly soon after, she met the love of her life, George Lewes, who was married but felt free to have affairs. His wife broke the terms of their open marriage arrangement by having three children with her lover.

Ms. Evans and Mr. Lewes were forced to go abroad since they were openly living together while not married. He feared she would lose any chance of having writing assignments accepted if they stayed. Back in England by March of 1855, Mr. Lewes took over as her literary agent, a new concept in the literary world. He obtained a legal separation from his wife in retaliation for her having deliberately incurred substantial debt as punishment for his abandoning her. This did not absolve him from responsibility for her debts. Mr. Lewes began to circulate Ms. Evans' manuscripts as having been written by a shy, but talented, friend of his. Ms. Evans realized it was time for her to have a *nom de plume*. She chose George in tribute to her lover, and Eliot from the name of a place she had seen on a local map in her father's office. Mr. Lewes continued to be aggressive in representing her by introducing new marketing concepts, a royalty system used today, and the kind of advertising commonly and contemporarily referred to as "hype."

It was at their summer house in Surrey that both Mr. Lewes and Ms. Evans met and welcomed John Cross into their lives as a beloved quasi-nephew. Ms. Evans had met John Cross in Rome on April 18, 1869, though she was already aquainted with the Cross family.

George Lewes became seriously ill and died on November 30,

1878. After the end of the mourning period for Mr. Lewes, Ms. Evans proposed to Mr. Cross, despite his being 20 years younger than she. A distraught Mr. Cross, finding no way to refuse, married Ms. Evans at St. George's Church on May 6, 1880. With Mr. Cross's history of mental illness and suicide attempts, this was not an easy marriage for the few months it endured.

Marian Evans Lewes Cross died of acute laryngitis on December 22, 1880 and was buried beside George Lewes.

Historical Background

Mary Ann Evans Lewes Cross lived in a time of new and revolutionary ideas. Raised with Evangelical piety under the influence of the principal governess, Maria Lewis, at Mrs. Wallington's School between 1828 and 1832, she was also influenced by Charles Bray, her neighbor in Coventry. He was a self-taught Freethinker (agnostic or one who doesn't know if God exists), and campaigned for radical causes. At the Brays' home, she was exposed to political ideology at variance with her father's Toryism, in addition to different religious views. Bray's extended family read Greek and German with Ms. Evans and discussed theology with her. From this and her own studying, she was able to present issues of morality and philosophy in her novels, which reflected nineteenth-century England's growing agnosticism, spiritual despair, and growing interest in psychology, history, and science.

At Charles Bray's home, Ms. Evans observed first hand an open marriage (both partners having agreed to the other having affairs), between Bray and his wife, Cara. George Sand (the *nom de plume* of Amandine Dudevant), through Ms. Evans' reading of her writing, led Ms. Evans to be anti-marriage in her youth. Later, Mr. Lewes registered his wife's child with Thorton Hunt under the Lewes surname, and remained friendly with both his wife and her lover, opening another view to Ms. Evans. The marriage laws were slanted so that a man could not be sued for divorce on the grounds of adultery unless his wife could prove "unnatural acts," but if his wife committed adultery, the husband had only to petition Parliament (at substantial cost) to obtain a divorce.

Not having the money for a divorce, Mr. Lewes and Ms. Evans defied the strict Victorian moral code by openly living together as husband and wife without benefit of clergy.

Writing was judged by the sex of the writer, and those who wanted to be taken seriously, such as George Eliot and Currer Bell (Charlotte Brontë), who were forced to take male names under which to publish. George Eliot's novels reflect traditional society (before the Reform Act of 1832), but they also show its evolution with the advent of the railroad and the new developments in medicine and public health.

Chronology of George Eliot's Works

1844–1846 translated Strauss's *Das Leben Jesu*

1852–1854 secret editor of *Westminster Review*

1854 translated Feuerbach's *Das Wesen des Christenthuns*

1855–1856 translated Spinoza's *Ethics*

1857 *Scenes of Clerical Life* published in *Blackwood's Magazine*

1859 *Adam Bede*

1859 short story: "The Lifted Veil"

1860 *The Mill on the Floss*

1861 *Silas Marner*

1862–1863 *Romola* published in *Cornhill Magazine*

1866 *Felix Holt the Radical*

1868 *The Spanish Gypsy*

1869–1871 poems: "How Lisa Loved the King," "Agatha," "The Legend of Jubal," and "Armgart"

1871–1872 *Middlemarch*

1876 *Daniel Deronda*

1879 essays: *Impressions of Theophrastus Such*

Master List of Characters

Dorothea Brooke (Dodo)—*Celia's older sister; married to Casaubon until his death, during which time she lived at Lowick Manor; later marries Ladislaw; lived with her uncle and sister at Brooke's home, Tipton Grange, until her marriage, at age 20, to Casaubon.*

Celia Brooke (Kitty)—*Dorothea's younger sister; marries Chettam and moves to his home, Freshitt Hall, after having lived with her uncle and sister at Tipton Grange; the mother of the baby, Arthur.*

Brooke—*Dorothea and Celia's uncle; member of the board of the new fever hospital; friend of Casaubon for more than ten years.*

Ladislaw—*Casaubon's second cousin; Dorothea's second husband; Bulstrode's secret step-grandson via Bulstrode's first wife; close friend of the Lydgates; works for Brooke; newly arrived to the area from Rome, where he had been studying art.*

Lydgate—*Innovative young doctor who is new to the area; studied medicine in Paris; marries Rosamond; befriends the also newly arrived Ladislaw; chief medical superintendent of the new hospital.*

Rosamond (Rosy)—*Daughter of Vincy; sister of Fred; married to Lydgate; niece through marriage of Bulstrode; niece of Featherstone.*

Bulstrode—*Banker; secret step-grandfather of Ladislaw via his first wife; head of the board of the new fever hospital; brother-in-law to Vincy via his wife, Harriet; uncle to Fred and Rosamond; calls his home "The Shrubs"; bought Stone Court from Joshua Rigg.*

Fred Vincy—*Son of the mayor; brother to Rosamond; in love with Mary; favored nephew of the rich and dying Featherstone.*

Joshua Rigg—*Inherits Featherstone's land, home (Stone Court), and most of his possessions, providing he add Featherstone to his name; probably Featherstone's son; sells Stone Court to Bulstrode.*

Mary Garth—*Caleb's daughter; beloved of Fred; niece and nurse of her uncle, the dying Featherstone (via her father's sister); insists Fred must sort out his own life before she will wed him.*

Mr. Vincy—*Manufacturer; the mayor; Fred and Rosamond's father; father-in-law of Lydgate; Bulstrode's brother-in-law.*

Farebrother—*Vincy's choice as chaplain for the new hospital; lives with his mother, aunt, and elder sister; eventually rents Lowick Manor; loves Mary but speaks to her in Fred's behalf.*

Caleb Garth—*Brother of Featherstone's first wife; father of Mary, Christy, Ben, Letty, Alfred, and Jim; Fred's employer; married to Susan; kind and caring, sometimes at the unintended expense of his own family.*

John Raffles—*Rigg's estranged stepfather; attempts to blackmail Bulstrode; is attended in his illness by Lydgate.*

Sir James Chettam—*First attracted to Dorothea; marries Celia; baby Arthur's father.*

Reverend Casaubon—*Marries the unsuspecting Dorothea more as a companion and secretary than as a wife; owns Lowick Manor; 27 years older than his bride.*

Mrs. Cadwallader—*Wife of the rector; oldest neighbor of Brooke; opposed to Dorothea's first marriage; opinionated and outspoken with her friends.*

Rector Cadwallader—*Refuses to intervene to postpone Dorothea and Casaubon's marriage when asked to do so by Chettam.*

Peter Featherstone—*Uncle to Rosamond, Fred, and Mary; Vincy's brother-in-law; dying; is besieged by relatives wanting to inherit his property.*

Tucker—*Curate of the church at Lowick Manor.*

Tykes—*Bulstrode's choice as chaplain of the new fever hospital, although the hospital lies in Farebrother's parish; Bulstrode expects Lydgate to vote for Tykes.*

Miss Noble—*Farebrother's aunt via his mother; lives with Farebrother, his mother, and his sister; takes a special liking to Ladislaw.*

Madame Laure—*Actress who successfully eludes punishment for murdering her husband onstage during Lydgate's years as a medical student in Paris; is loved by Lydgate but refuses his offer of marriage.*

Tantripp—*Dorothea and Celia's maid; came to Brooke's home with them when their mother died.*

Naumann—*Ladislaw's German art teacher and friend who is in Italy with him.*

Bambridge—*Horse trader to whom Fred is in debt.*

Mrs. Plymdale—*Ned's mother; friend of Rosamond's aunt, Mrs. Bulstrode.*

Trumbull—*Second cousin of Featherstone who inherits his gold-headed cane; auctioneer.*

Diamond—*Horse that Fred plans to buy cheaply and sell at a profit to repay debt.*

Wrench—*Doctor attending the Vincys until he misdiagnoses the seriousness of Fred's illness.*

Sir Lydgate—*Lydgate's baronet uncle.*

Dagley—*One of Brooke's tenants.*

Nancy Nash—*Patient whose misdiagnosed illness Lydgate treated.*

Sarah Dunkirk Ladislaw—*Ladislaw's mother; Bulstrode's step-daughter.*

Captain Lydgate—*Lydgate's cousin; son of Sir Lydgate.*

Toller, Minchen, and Chichely—*Lydgate's opposition in Middle-march.*

Standish—*Featherstone's lawyer.*

Mrs. Abel—*Bulstrode's servant at Stone Court.*

Hawley—*Lawyer who attempts to verify the rumors concerning Bulstrode and Raffles.*

Martha—*The Lydgates' maid.*

Ned Plymdale—*Rosamond's former suitor.*

Hopkins—*The undertaker who buried Raffles.*

Mrs. Waule—*Featherstone's sister.*

Summary of the Novel

Dorothea Brooks, a pious young woman, lives with her younger sister and uncle at Tipton Grange. She thinks she is in love with a deeply intellectual older man, Casaubon. After marrying him, she discovers he is not what she wanted nor is the marriage, but it is what she has. Her husband's second cousin, Ladislaw, visits them on their honeymoon trip, innocently prompting jealousy in the older man. Casaubon adds a codicil to his will that requires his young widow to relinquish the substantial money and property he will leave her should she marry Ladislaw at any time after his death. He dies soon after.

Rosamond Vincy is taken with the new young doctor, Lydgate, who thinks he does not yet have the right to marry because he hasn't made his fortune. He had been studying innovations in medicine in Paris, and has come to Middlemarch to head the new fever hospital (an unpaid position) and attempt to build the practice he has bought. She marries him, and manages to spend them into debt. Instead of being supportive when their debts come due, she keeps her thoughts to herself. She seeks separation—first from their problems and then from her husband.

It is the widowed Dorothea, after accidentally finding Rosamond unchaperoned with Ladislaw, who explains to her that Rosamond and Lydgate must talk with each other and endure their problems together. Unbeknownst to Dorothea, Rosamond has fantasies concerning Ladislaw as her resource. Dorothea thinks that Ladislaw prefers Rosamond. Dorothea did not hear him say she is the only woman he loves when she came upon them together, alone, in Lydgate's home.

Fred Vincy has failed his exams rather than graduate and be forced to become a member of the clergy by his father. Mary explains that she would not marry him if he became a clergyman when he didn't want to. She also would not marry a man devoted to gambling and hunting. He'd already asked Caleb, Mary's father, to co-sign a loan to pay a gambling debt. He lost the money to repay the loan on a bad horse trade. Mary could not have such irresponsibility in a husband, and she is very upset that her father must now repay Fred's gambling debt. After an illness, much angst, and a return to school for his degree, Fred realizes he would like to do what Mary's father does—manage estates—and he works with Caleb, learning the trade.

Ladislaw has come to Middlemarch to be near Dorothea. While respectful of her marriage to his second cousin (who had been supporting him as a familial duty), he was falling in love with her. Her husband had ordered her not to invite him to their home, but her uncle—Brooke—hired him to help at Tipton Grange and they did run into each other. Ladislaw hears of the codicil to Casaubon's will and vows to leave Dorothea in peace. It takes him over two months to actually leave. He later returns. After being found by Dorothea with his hands intimately on Rosamond's face, he vows to leave again rather than have Dorothea penniless. She doesn't want that, and tells him. They marry.

Bulstrode, head of the board of directors at the new fever hospital, had been married before to the daughter of a questionable family, which just happened to be Ladislaw's mother's family. Before being married, Bulstrode had hired Raffles to find Ladislaw's mother, who had run away to the stage. He'd done this at Ladislaw's grandmother's request, so that her daughter could inherit the business from her deceased father (Bulstrode's first wife's first husband) before she gave it to Bulstrode upon their marriage. Raffles did find the girl, but Bulstrode managed to suppress this information. Raffles shows up at Stone Court to attempt to gain an income from his estranged stepson, who has just inherited Featherstone's home, but Riggs refuses him. Raffles recognized Bulstrode and renewed his blackmailing of him. Later, Raffles becomes ill and asks to be taken to Bulstrode's home, where Lydgate comes to attend him.

Bulstrode does not follow Lydgate's medical instructions, Raffles dies, and Lydgate is under suspicion until Dorothea clears the matter and his reputation. Lydgate realizes people think the 1,000 pound loan he took from Bulstrode was a bribe to "hush" the murder of Raffles. He accepted a loan from Dorothea to cover the debt and cut all communication with Bulstrode. Caleb, whom Bulstrode had attempted to engage to manage his estate while he fled his disgrace, also refused to have any dealings with Bulstrode.

Estimated Reading Time

Middlemarch will take approximately 26 hours to read. The book may easily be broken into the parts designated by the author. The Prelude and Book One will take approximately three and a half hours to read; Book Two—three hours; Book Three—two hours; Book Four—three and a half hours; Book Five—four hours; Book Six—three and a half hours; Book Seven—three and a half hours; and Book Eight and the Finale—three hours.

Each person reading the book will find some sections more interesting than others and will choose to spend more time on them. The original was printed in several issues of a magazine, and the book was not designed to be read in one marathon session. Do not allow the length of time necessary to read the book to diminish your enjoyment of the novel.

Prelude and Book One: Miss Brooke

Prelude and Chapters 1–6

New Characters:

Dorothea: *20-year-old, serious, studious, religious older sister of Celia and niece of Brooke, in whose home, Tipton Grange, both girls live*

Celia: *the younger, more fun-loving sister of Dorothea and niece of Brooke*

Brooke: *the 60-year-old uncle of both Dorothea and Celia, who brought the girls to live with him when their mother died a year ago, is considering running for Parliament*

Casaubon: *a 47-year-old scholar who lives in Lowick Manor and has been Brooke's friend for about ten years*

Chettam: *the young baronet who loves Dorothea, not realizing she does not return his love, living at Freshitt Hall*

Mrs. Cadwallader: *the rector's wife who is a neighbor to Brooke*

Summary

Celia asks Dorothea to divide the jewelry their mother has left them. Their dinner guests, Chettam and Casaubon, discuss farming techniques, religion, and politics in an attempt to engage

Dorothea's attention, but Dorothea thinks Chettam should be interested in Celia. The next morning, Casaubon speaks to Dorothea of his loneliness. She begins to feel he may be thinking of marrying her, which she sees as a means to further her studies. After he leaves, Dorothea wanders through the woods with her dog. Chettam finds her to give her a puppy she doesn't want. She suggests he give the puppy to Celia. They discuss Dorothea's plan for new cottages, which Chettam declares he would like to build on his land.

Casaubon visits twice, each time seeming to disregard Dorothea's plan for cottages, much to her dismay. Brooke is invited to Lowick Manor, Casaubon's home, for several days. Chettam increases his own visits, but Dorothea continues to regard him as a potential brother-in-law, and to believe he thinks of her as a potential sister-in-law. Celia attempts to apprise her sister of Chettam's feelings, to no avail. Brooke returns with a marriage proposal for Dorothea. He also tells her he thinks Chettam would like to marry her. When she rejects this thought, Brooke reminds her how much older Casaubon is than she.

When it is clear she prefers Casaubon, Brooke gives Dorothea the letter from Casaubon. She writes him a note of acceptance and tells her uncle. He once again wonders if Chettam might not be the better husband for her. Before Casaubon comes to dinner the next evening, Dorothea tells her sister of the impending marriage. Celia is chagrined, but accepts the inevitable. Casaubon and Dorothea plan to marry in six weeks.

Mrs. Cadwallader arrives, argues politics with Brooke, and is upset when Celia tells her it is Casaubon—not Chettam—Dorothea will be marrying. When Mrs. Cadwallader tells Chettam, they agree Casaubon is much too old for Dorothea.

Analysis

We immediately see how misconceptions change the characters' lives. Dorothea thinks Chettam sees her as a potential sister-in-law, not wife. She treats him as she would a brother-in-law. He is interested in marrying her, so he sees this sisterly concern as the beginnings of love. When told by Celia that Chettam loves her, Dorothea thinks that is absurd. She has already married him to

Celia in her mind. Celia, assuming that Chettam and Dorothea will marry, says nothing of her feeling that Chettam and Dorothea are mismatched until after Dorothea has announced her engagement to Casaubon. While Dorothea had been viewing Chettam as a potential brother-in-law, so had Celia.

In addition, Dorothea seems to have some rigidly defined ideas of who each person is. She makes it very clear that Chettam should marry Celia, even before announcing her own impending marriage. She judges the older Casaubon as substantial and someone who she could not match intellectually unless she studied in many areas. He has only been quieter than the others and intimated his loneliness to her. She has been painting a mental image of their married love, which seems to have very little space in it for Casaubon to be anything other than what Dorothea expects: a scholar whom she will read to and aid in his studies. Only Mrs. Cadwallader and Chettam seem to see clearly that Casaubon is far too old and dry for Dorothea and that Chettam would be a better match.

Dorothea's choice of Casaubon over Chettam and Mrs. Cadwallader's protests have to do with the politic climate of the actual time when the story takes place. Dorothea is an Evangelist, a dissenter from the Church of England; Casaubon seems to be heading for a position as a bishop in the Church of England. Religion and government had been one in England until the Reform Bill of 1832, which repealed the law that seats in Parliament could only be held by members of the Church of England. Brooke—a Protestant—is thinking of standing for Parliament, and the niece he treats as a daughter is going to marry an Anglican. Mrs. Cadwallader apparently objects to more than Casaubon's age.

Study Questions

1. What is the reason Celia wants to divide their deceased mother's jewelry with Dorothea?

2. Who are the guests at dinner?

3. What gift does Chettam bring Dorothea?

4. What does Brooke bring Dorothea from his visit to Casaubon?

5. For what purpose does Casaubon want to marry Dorothea?

6. What is Dorothea's reason for marrying Casaubon?

7. What attempts does Brooke make to dissuade Dorothea from her decision?

8. In what way does Dorothea respond to Casaubon's proposal?

9. In what manner does Chettam express his dismay at Dorothea's engagement?

10. Why is Mrs. Cadwallader so disappointed in Dorothea's choice?

Answers

1. Celia would like to wear some of the jewelry left to her and her sister by their mother. Certain pieces would now be acceptable even to the most religious people. At Dorothea's request, they put the jewelry box away, upon receiving it, six months ago.

2. Brooke's dinner guests at Tipton Grange are to be Chettam—a young baronet and neighbor who is in love with Dorothea—and Casaubon, Brooke's old friend and near contemporary.

3. Chettam brings Dorothea a small, white Maltese puppy. She suggests he give the puppy to Celia.

4. Brooke brings some religious pamphlets, a letter to Dorothea, and a marriage proposal from his visit to Casaubon.

5. Casaubon wants to marry Dorothea because he wants a devoted and intellectual companion. His conversations with her have convinced him she will be charming and helpful in ending his loneliness and in aiding him with his work.

6. Dorothea feels it would be an honor to be Casaubon's companion. She sees him as an older man who would be able to help her formulate her own opinions. She wants the opportunity to learn from him.

7. Brooke tries to dissuade Dorothea from her decision to marry Casaubon by reminding her he is 27 years her senior and a moper. He prefers his books over people. Brooke won-

ders that he has known Casaubon for almost ten years but still doesn't know his ideas. Brooke also worries about Casaubon's health.

8. Dorothea accepts Casaubon's proposal with gratitude and great hopes for happiness once they are wed. She admires him and wants to learn from him. She believes marrying a scholar would be good for her.

9. Chettam expresses his dismay at Dorothea's engagement by becoming outraged and disgusted that her uncle would allow her to marry such an old man who is so boringly scholarly. He observes to Mrs. Cadwallader that Dorothea's friends should attempt to intervene. Brooke obviously will not.

10. Mrs. Cadwallader indicates her disappointment by telling Chettam how inappropriate it would have been for him to marry Dorothea when it is patently clear that his temperament is much more suited to marriage with Celia.

Suggested Essay Topics

1. Dorothea and Celia, although sisters, have exceedingly different views of life. Use the text to support this statement.

2. How may Dorothea's decision to marry Casaubon be seen as a political statement concerning the Reform Bill and religion?

Chapters 7–12

New Characters:

Ladislaw: *Casaubon's second cousin via his mother's sister, visiting from journeys abroad to study art, financed by Casaubon*

Lydgate: *newly arrived from studying medicine in Paris, he has bought Peacock's medical practice and is to be the medical superintendent of the new fever hospital*

Rosamond: *Fred's sister who has declined to nurse her dying uncle and would prefer to marry someone who is not from Middlemarch*

Fred: *Rosamond's playboy brother who is the favorite nephew of the rich and dying Featherstone*

Vincy: *a manufacturer and the mayor of Middlemarch who is the father of Fred, Bob, and Rosamond; Featherstone's brother-in-law through Featherstone's deceased second wife who was Mr. Vincy's wife's sister*

Featherstone: *Rosamond's and Fred's uncle and Vincy's brother-in-law, rich and dying, who leads his favorite nephew, Fred, to believe he will be his heir*

Mary: *the 22-year-old young woman who is nursing Featherstone and is his niece via his deceased first wife*

Cadwallader: *the rector (priest directing a church with no pastor) at Tipton Grange; Mrs. Cadwallader's husband; refuses to intervene in preventing Dorothea's engagement to Casaubon when requested to do so by Chettam*

Tucker: *the curate (clergyman in charge) of the church at Lowick Manor, Casaubon's home*

Bulstrode: *the banker who is both married to Vincy's sister and is the Vincy children's uncle*

Mrs. Waule: *Featherstone's sister who is looking for an inheritance from him*

Summary

Dorothea wants to prepare for her marriage by learning to read Latin and Greek. Casaubon wants her to learn to write these languages. He teaches her several disciplines, despite her uncle's protests that these are too taxing for a woman. Brooke is delighted that Casaubon may become a bishop, and more readily accepts the marriage than his neighbors do. Chettam continues his visits and becomes so distraught at seeing Casaubon and Dorothea together that he asks Cadwallader to intervene.

Dorothea, her sister, and uncle visit her new home. Casaubon asks her to choose her room but she prefers all such decisions be made for her. She refuses to even discuss making changes in the house. She discovers a picture of Casaubon's aunt and asks about

it; Casaubon declines to discuss her except to say she'd made an unfortunate marriage. Brooke urges Dorothea to see the Lowick cottages, church, and village. On their way to Lowick, Celia sees a young artist and tells Dorothea. Tucker gives them a guided tour. Dorothea admits to Casaubon that she is a little disappointed there is not much for her to do to better the area.

Ladislaw joins them and is introduced as Casaubon's cousin (although he is actually a second cousin). As they discuss art, Brooke invites him to Tipton Grange to see his own art. Upon questioning, Casaubon divulges that he supports Ladislaw, who will travel abroad to study art for an additional year. Dorothea thinks this is admirable of Casaubon. Ladislaw leaves without making the promised visit to Tipton Grange. Dorothea and Casaubon plan their honeymoon trip. Casaubon is very concerned that Celia declines to accompany them as Dorothea's companion. Dorothea is annoyed that he thinks she would need a companion. During a celebratory dinner party at Tipton Grange, the neighboring women gossip about Casaubon's declining health, Dorothea and Chettam being better suited to each other than Dorothea and her fiancé, whether Celia and Chettam will marry now that Dorothea is engaged, and Lydgate.

At the Vincys', Rosamond and her mother chat as first Fred, then Vincy appear for breakfast. Fred is questioned about Lydgate. Rosamond is chided for not nursing her dying uncle. The next day, Fred and Rosamond visit their uncle, Featherstone, only to find most of his siblings (or their representatives) there to see him die. He refuses to see any of them, but calls Fred to his side and gives him a gift of money. He demands that Fred get him a letter from Bulstrode stating Fred has not been using the promise of an inheritance as collateral for debts. Mary is staying at Stone Court to nurse her uncle, and visits with Rosamond. Just before Fred and Rosamond leave, Lydgate arrives to attend to Featherstone. Rosamond and Fred are mostly silent, each lost in thought, on the ride home.

Analysis

The meanness of the characters is taken in stride as "business as usual," according to the narrator's view. Mrs. Vincy is convinced

Mary is nursing Featherstone in his terminal illness in order to have some inheritance from him. Mrs. Vincy also chides Rosamond for not nursing her uncle, which could have gained her some small inheritance. Mrs. Waule makes a point of bringing to her dying brother's attention the rumor of Fred's relying on his expected inheritance in order to secure loans. Featherstone plays a sort of psychological game with Fred by demanding he bring a letter from Bulstrode declaring there was no attempt by Fred to gain loans on the promise of his inheritance from Featherstone. None of these people is particularly shocked by the actions of the others, only dismayed at the situations in which they find themselves.

Money is an issue; Vincy is not only the mayor but a business-man who is in a financial bind due to the upheavals in govern-ment at this time. With the Whigs and the Tories polarized by the religious issues of the Reform Act and the economic depression after the French Revolution, businesses were suffering. Vincy sent his son to school when he could ill afford it, and that money must be recouped, even if by Rosamond nursing Featherstone.

At the same time, these people are fairly ignorant of what others are thinking or feeling. Casaubon thinks he is being kind when he wants Celia to accompany them on their honeymoon. Dorothea will not be alone while he pursues his scholarly works, he thinks. Dorothea wants to do this work with him, and thinks he feels he will be disturbed in his work by her. Rosamond thinks Fred is "horrid." He has been educated to be a clergyman at his father's insistence and extra expense, but refuses to graduate. He does not want to follow this profession. Fred, however, knows he is not suited for the ministry and cannot enter it. He must fail his exams (which means wasting his father's money in an economic depression) in order to avoid being forced into becoming a clergyman. When Mary defends Fred for his refusal, Rosamond assumes this is nothing more than an expression of Mary's long-standing love for Fred.

Mrs. Vincy cannot abide her thought that Mary—whose father is only an estate manager—is pursuing Fred. Mary is not pursuing Fred, because she wants him to straighten out his affairs to his own satisfaction before she acts upon their mutual love. He, in turn, is very upset that she will not marry him—despite his not having asked her and his having no way to support her. There seems to be some kind of vacuum in their lives which is filled only by thinking for another and then acting upon these thoughts as if they really were those of the other person.

Study Questions

1. What is the first indication that Dorothea and Casaubon may have decided to marry too hastily?

2. For what reasons does Brooke allow Dorothea to accept Casaubon's proposal?

3. What is Chettam's purpose in asking Cadwallader to intervene?

4. When do Dorothea and Ladislaw first meet?

5. Why is Tucker answering all the questions about Lowick?

6. What is Mrs. Vincy's argument against Mary?

7. How are both the Vincys and the Garths related to Featherstone?

8. Why are all Featherstone's siblings gathered at Stone Court?

9. What is it that Featherstone discusses with Fred?

10. What evidence do we have that Rosamond and Lydgate are falling in love?

Answers

1. During her six-week engagement, Dorothea wants to learn to read Greek and Latin so that, once she is married, she may read to Casaubon in order to save his failing eyesight. He wants her to learn to write these languages, which indicates he would prefer to do the reading himself, alone.

2. Brooke is delighted that Casaubon may become a bishop and has money. He offers several reasons for Dorothea not to marry Casaubon, but she refutes each. She prefers a scholarly existence and thinks to have one as Casaubon's wife. She has always seemed to know her opinion. Brooke feels he cannot object to her having what it is she thinks she wants: marriage to Casaubon.

3. Chettam asks Cadwallader to intervene because Mrs. Cadwallader will not. Chettam had been courting Dorothea and knows of her desire to make improvements. He is also worried that Casaubon is too old and does not have enough life left in him. He wants Mr. Cadwallader to tell Brooke to make Dorothea wait until she is older.

4. Dorothea, Celia, and Brooke go to Lowick Manor to see where Dorothea will be living. As they walk around the village and to the church, Celia sees a young man who Casaubon explains is his second cousin; this is Ladislaw.

5. Tucker is the curate of the church. As such, he knows more about it and the village than Casaubon does.

6. Mrs. Vincy is terribly worried that Mary, who is poor, will marry her son, Fred, to have a steady income.

7. Featherstone is an old, childless man who has been widowed twice: the first time by Mary's aunt (her father's sister), and the second time by Mrs. Vincy's sister

8. The siblings are gathered at Stone Court because Featherstone is rich and he is dying. This is their last chance to have him include them in his will. They suspect they are not already there.

9. Featherstone was told the rumor that Fred has run up debts by intimating that he will be Featherstone's heir and will soon have all that is Featherstone's.

10. Rosamond asks Fred to take her riding when she knows he will visit Stone Court, where Lydgate is her uncle's doctor. Once there, Lydgate and she cannot keep their eyes from each another.

Suggested Essay Topics

1. Both Mary and Rosamond are Featherstone's nieces. Compare their attitudes toward their rich, dying uncle with their attitudes toward the men they love—in Mary's case, Fred, and in Rosamond's, Lydgate.

2. Only Chettam strenuously objects to Dorothea's impending marriage. Brooke, Celia, and Mrs. Cadwallader all feel this is not the match for her. Explain their reasons for not fighting against the marriage.

SECTION THREE

Book Two:
Old and Young

Chapters 13–18

New Characters:

Farebrother: *a vicar who could become the chaplain of the new hospital*

Tyke: *Bulstrode's choice for the chaplaincy of the new hospital*

Miss Noble: *the sister of Farebrother's mother; lives with Farebrother, his mother, and sister Winifred*

Madame Laure: *the actress who murdered her husband onstage and is the one woman Lydgate has loved in the past*

Summary

Bulstrode and Lydgate meet at the bank to discuss the new fever hospital. Bulstrode makes it clear to Lydgate that he wants Tyke, not Farebrother, to be its chaplain. Vincy has already arrived to ask Bulstrode for the letter Featherstone wants from Fred. After consulting with his wife, Bulstrode writes the letter, which Fred then brings to Featherstone, who questions its wording yet makes a gift of 100 pounds to Fred. After demeaning Fred's father, Featherstone allows the letter to be burned. Fred then has a discussion with Mary; she maintains she cannot marry a man who is in debt and will not work.

Lydgate has studied in Paris, and has adopted the Parisian practice of not filling his own prescriptions. He is interested in medical science and wants to reform present practices. When he was studying, he fell in love with an actress, Madame Laure, who murdered her husband onstage as they acted out a murder scene. She was released from custody when the investigators thought a slip of her foot caused the knife to enter her husband's flesh. The couple had seemed to be in love. When Lydgate proposed to her, she told him the truth and declared she wanted no more husbands. This convinced him to avoid women except scientifically, but no one in Middlemarch knows of this part of his past.

At Vincy's, there is a heated discussion about who the new hospital's chaplain shall be. The guests attempt to draw Lydgate into the debate, but he declines. The high point of the evening for him is the conversation with Rosamond. Farebrother arrives and commences a game of whist (cards). Lydgate considers this a waste of time, but he becomes interested in watching Farebrother win. As Lydgate leaves, he is aware that Rosamond has just as much interest in him as he has in her. He doesn't plan to marry for at least five years, having just bought a practice. That left him with little funds. Rosamond has not yet realized his financial condition.

Lydgate visits Farebrother, Farebrother's sister (Winifred), mother, and aunt (Miss Noble) the next evening. After talking with the ladies, the two men retire to the vicar's (a clergyman who receives a stipend but not the tithes of his church) study. Farebrother shows Lydgate his entomological collection. Farebrother mentions that if Lydgate votes for him in the matter of the new chaplain, he will surely offend Bulstrode. Farebrother and Bulstrode are of different parties. Farebrother would not be offended if Lydgate votes for Bulstrode's choice.

Lydgate realizes Farebrother plays cards and billiards in order to win money through betting. Farebrother enjoys doing so. Lydgate finds this hurts the possibility of his giving Farebrother his vote. He knows the 40 pounds salary would help Farebrother. When the board of the new hospital meets, there is heated debate about Farebrother and Tyke. The vote proceeds and Lydgate is left with the deciding vote. Told he is expected to vote as Bulstrode dictates, Lydgate votes for Tyke. Lydgate is unsure if he voted for the right man. Farebrother treats him just as he had before the vote was taken.

Analysis

The politics of what Lydgate thought to be a simple little country town are beginning to become apparent to him. He thinks Farebrother may be the best choice for the chaplaincy of the new hospital. Farebrother himself has explained that Lydgate must vote for the choice of the man who brought him into the hospital as the chief medical superintendent. That man, Bulstrode, favors Tyke, so that is who Lydgate must vote for. It nags at Lydgate that this is exactly what he does. He protests that he is doing so because Tyke is the right choice—not because he is Bulstrode's candidate.

There are other issues, too. Rosamond is in love with the idea of a relationship with Lydgate, not with the man himself. He is still too new to the area to know this, though there may be suspicion among her mother and her aunt. She has decided she cannot marry the Middlemarch men because they don't belong to a high enough class for her. Lydgate is a doctor, affiliated in a high position with the new hospital (unpaid), and has an interest in medical research. This adds up to being respected as his wife, to her way of thinking. Rosamond does not stop to think of finances as the potential wife of a struggling young doctor must; that is not part of the picture she has painted for herself as his wife.

There is a parallel to governmental politics here. Should the Reform Act pass, the middle class would become partners with the aristocracy. Boroughs would be reapportioned according to new definitions of who could or could not vote. The members of Parliament for each borough would be reapportioned. The bill was considered almost radical, as is Rosamond's behavior in aligning herself with an unknown—Lydgate—just as the aristocracy had to align itself with the unknown—the middle class.

Study Questions

1. Why does Bulstrode mention Tyke in discussing the new fever hospital with Lydgate?

2. What is Farebrother's rationale for disliking Bulstrode?

3. Explain Bulstrode's reluctance to write the letter Featherstone requested.

4. How are Lydgate and Farebrother alike?

5. What need is there for Farebrother to play whist and billiards?

6. Why is Lydgate determined to avoid romantic attachments?

7. What are Mary's objections to marrying Fred?

8. What are Lydgate's reasons for voting for Tyke?

9. How would you summarize the debate about coroners at Vincy's dinner party?

10. As a mother, what does Mrs. Farebrother have to say about her son?

Answers

1. Bulstrode mentions Tyke because the new hospital is to be located in Farebrother's parish. Bulstrode wants no other spiritual guide than Tyke to have the chaplaincy of the hospital.

2. Farebrother thinks Bulstrode dislikes him due to their being of different parties. Bulstrode and his cronies adopt a "holier-than-thou" attitude towards those not of their party.

3. Bulstrode thinks Fred borrowed money on the promise of Featherstone's inheritance, as Mrs. Waule reported. Bulstrode thinks it will curb his nephew's extravagance and strengthen his character if he doesn't write the letter.

4. Lydgate and Farebrother both enjoy scientific pursuits; they both enjoy the entomological collection. They also both knew Trawley, who shared an apartment in Paris with Lydgate and was a correspondent of Farebrother's.

5. Farebrother is a vicar of the church. This means he is paid a stipend. He doesn't share in the tithes. This leaves him with very little money. By gambling and winning at cards and billiards, he earns the rest of the money necessary to support himself, his sister, his aunt, and his mother.

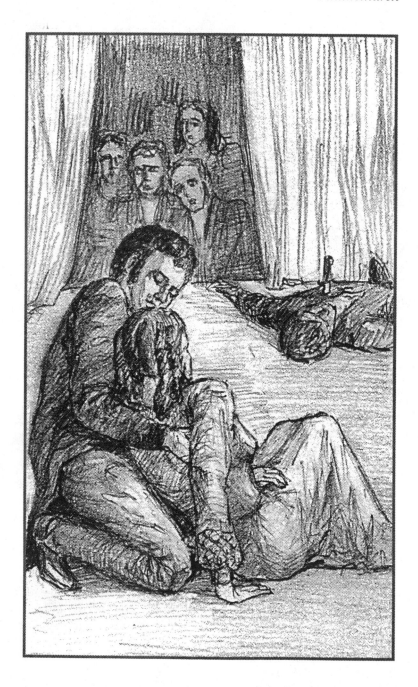

6. When Lydgate was studying medicine in Paris, he fell in love with a married actress who murdered her husband during a death scene onstage. When he proposed, she admitted her guilt and refused his offer. He decided not to become involved with women after that.

7. Fred's father sent him to school to become a clergyman, an expense Vincy really couldn't afford. Not wanting to be a clergyman, Fred failed his exams rather than graduate and be forced into the profession. Now he hunts and gambles and idles away the day. Mary doesn't want him to hypocritically become a clergyman, but she doesn't want a gambling loafer for a husband, either.

8. Lydgate votes for Tyke for a number of reasons: Bulstrode expects him to cooperate in the vote, Farebrother explained he would not be offended by Lydgate's choice, and he was simply not certain which of the two clergymen was the right choice.

9. The traditional view of the issue, held by Chichely (who was his Majesty's coroner) and Vincy, is that coroners should be lawyers who recognize evidence and do postmortems. Lydgate adheres to the view that a doctor as coroner can make medical decisions about the cause of death.

10. Mrs. Farebrother thinks her son undervalues himself. This is unacceptable, because he is then undervaluing God, who made him the man he is. She also thinks her son is an excellent preacher.

Suggested Essay Topics

1. Bulstrode thinks it may strengthen Fred's character not to give him the letter Featherstone demanded. Do you agree or disagree with Bulstrode's reasoning? Why?

2. A vicar is a clergyman. Gambling, cards, and billiards are not usually approved by the church. How is it possible for Farebrother, a vicar, to openly gamble at cards and billiards?

Chapters 19–22

New Characters:

Naumann: *Ladislaw's German art teacher and friend, with whom he lives in Rome*

Tantripp: *Celia and Dorothea's longtime maid, who accompanies Dorothea on her honeymoon*

Summary

Ladislaw and Naumann come across Dorothea in the Vatican, where Casaubon has just left her. Naumann wants Ladislaw to speak to her about sitting for a portrait, but Ladislaw explains she is on her honeymoon and has just married his second cousin. Naumann insists. Dorothea is upset that Casaubon is not affectionate, and he does not want her to help him with his work. They argued before separating for the day.

Ladislaw visits them when Casaubon is not home. Dorothea entertains him alone. She mentions Casaubon is usually away all day, which confounds Ladislaw. They discover that when they first met at Lowick Manor, Dorothea was not criticizing Ladislaw's art. She was commenting on her lack of knowledge about art. It becomes apparent that Ladislaw has his differences with Casaubon. Casaubon arrives and is not pleased at finding Ladislaw alone with Dorothea. After Ladislaw leaves, Dorothea apologizes to Casaubon for their earlier argument. She asks his forgiveness, which he does not grant.

The next day, Ladislaw joins the Casaubons for dinner. He suggests a tour of artists' studios the following day. One of these is Naumann's, where Naumann asks Casaubon to sit for a sketch for a painting of St. Thomas Aquinas. Although surprised, Casaubon agrees. They begin immediately, with all four conversing as the sketching proceeds. Ladislaw falls even further under Dorothea's spell and plots to see her alone again. He calls in the middle of the day, when he knows Casaubon will not be there. Dorothea asks his advice about cameos. She wants to bring one home to Celia. The talk turns to her desire to do good works. They argue about Casaubon's work and his methodology. Ladislaw declares he will

not come again, thinking she dislikes him. She tells him she and Casaubon would be delighted to see him again and that she does like him. As before, he meets Casaubon on his way out. Dorothea informs Casaubon that Ladislaw will no longer be taking his money, but will be earning his own.

Analysis

Reality comes quickly and brutally to Dorothea's marriage. Now she understands why Casaubon had wanted Celia to accompany them on their honeymoon. Now she is glad of Tantripp's company. She has a husband who does his work alone all day on their honeymoon. He is not affectionate toward her, nor even generous in spirit. His first priority is his research on his book, which he does in a solitary, languid manner. He invites no company, no aid, no interruptions—even from his young, eager, intelligent, new wife. She becomes angry, but one cannot help wonder if she is angry at who he is or at herself for seeing him only as who she wanted him to be.

Ladislaw, also, seems to be a mass of raw nerves. He rankles at the mention of his second cousin's name, although he has lived at Casaubon's expense most of his life. It seems that Casaubon has "done the right thing," but with no good intent behind it other than to have done the right thing. Ladislaw is dumbfounded that Casaubon would leave Dorothea alone all day on their honeymoon. He cannot say anything about it to her. She doesn't seem to realize this is most unusual. He forcibly tells Naumann not to refer to her as his aunt, but cannot see for himself just how taken he is with her. He has studied art for years, yet tells Dorothea that this cannot be his life. It is too one-sided. He declares he will no longer take his second cousin's money, but has no idea how he will earn his own. These contradictions in his life seemed to be based upon his swiftly changing feelings, especially those toward Dorothea.

Dorothea's and Ladislaw's swiftly changing feelings mirror the swift changes in the government at that time. Due to The Reform Bill, Anglicans (members of the Church of England) would no longer be the only ones permitted to hold seats in Parliament. This encompassed not only a change in the religious beliefs of the country's elected leaders, but also a change in the economic structure of the government. The laws concerning who could or could not vote became more liberal. The middle class and other religions would now also be represented in Parliament. These representatives would pursue the interests of those who elected them. Casaubon seems to be symbolic of the presently ruling aristocracy. Ladislaw seems to be repudiating his rule.

Study Questions

1. Why is Dorothea at the Vatican?

2. What is Naumann's reaction when he first sees Dorothea?

3. How does Ladislaw respond to Naumann on seeing Dorothea?

4. For what reason does Ladislaw refuse to ask Dorothea to sit for the portrait?

5. When she is alone, why does Dorothea sob?

6. What is it that prompts the argument between the Casaubons?

7. How would you describe the differences between Ladislaw's and Casaubon's outlooks on the world?

8. What is the purpose of Ladislaw's offer to return the next day?

9. For what reason does Ladislaw refer to Casaubon's refusal to learn German?

10. What prompts Ladislaw to say he will not come again?

Answers

1. Dorothea is in the sixth week of her honeymoon in Rome with Casaubon. She is looking at art while he pursues his studies at the Vatican.

2. When Naumann first sees Dorothea, he runs to find Ladislaw to show him this example of beauty in life and convince him that the rich, older husband will certainly pay handsomely for her portrait.

3. Ladislaw tells Naumann that she will not want to be painted and that she is married to his second cousin. They argue

, because of Naumann's single-minded failure to understand why anyone would not want to be painted by him.

4. Ladislaw doesn't want to ask her to sit for the portrait because Naumann puts too much into his paintings, seeing his subjects too grandiosely and too intimately at the same time.

5. Dorothea realizes her idealized picture of what her marriage would be like is not the reality of it. Casaubon does not want her company nor her aid in writing his works. He is not aware of her need for some small show of affection, nor is he aware that she genuinely desires to work beside him.

6. Dorothea rankles at Casaubon's refusal of her offers to help him in his work, thinking he rejects her. He, in turn, thinks she is attempting to spy on the progress of his work when she tells him she wants to work with him.

7. Casaubon seems to view the world as a scholarly work to be studied and observed, but not lived. Ladislaw, on the other hand, rejects even his art if it means he is to view, rather than live, life.

8. Ladislaw offers to return the next day because it is unseemly for him to pay a visit without Casaubon's presence. It is obvious that Dorothea has been crying.

9. Ladislaw is angry that Dorothea worships his second cousin and wants to present some flaw in his character. He refers to Casaubon's refusal to learn German, which is mandatory in order to read certain documents.

10. Ladislaw goes to see Dorothea in the middle of the day, when he knows Casaubon will not be there. He and Dorothea quarrel. He tells her he will not come again since she dislikes him.

Suggested Essay Topics

1. Reform is one of the problems Lydgate is having trouble with since his move to Middlemarch. Explain this statement in view of both his medical practices and his new place in Middlemarch's society.

2. Dorothea has planned her marriage without taking her husband's personality into account. In what ways has he turned out to be different from the husband she thought he would be?

Book Three: Waiting for Death

Chapters 23–28

New Characters:

Ned Plymdale: *Rosamond's former suitor*

Bambridge: *the horse trader to whom Fred is in debt*

Mrs. Garth: *the educated wife of Caleb, mother of Mary and several other children, who takes in students to earn money for her own son, Alfred's, tuition*

Diamond: *the horse who lamed himself; Fred, his new owner, is unable to repay the debt for which Caleb co-signed*

Wrench: *the Vincy family doctor until Lydgate is called in to treat Fred*

Caleb: *Mrs. Garth's husband, Mary's father, and Featherstone's brother-in-law through Featherstone's marriage to Caleb's now deceased sister; also the co-signer of Fred's loan*

Summary

Fred is in debt to Bambridge for 160 pounds. After being unable to repay his note as promised, without telling Mrs. Garth, he asked Caleb to co-sign the note. He didn't want to go to his own father for the money. Fred retrieves 80 pounds he'd deposited with

his mother (from the gift of 100 pounds Featherstone had given him) to add to the trade of his horse to buy a superior horse at the fair. Once in possession of Diamond, the new horse, he intends to sell the animal for a profit. He plans to use the money remaining from what his uncle gave him plus the profits from Diamond toward repaying the debt. However, Diamond manages to lame himself before Fred has the opportunity to sell him.

Fred goes to the Garth's home to confess that he cannot repay the loan. Caleb is not to be found, but Mrs. Garth is there. When Caleb returns, Fred tells them. Caleb says it is a bad time for them to lose extra money. Mrs. Garth is angry—both at the loss of the money and at not having been told of the co-signing of the note in the first place. They will have to use their savings, Alfred's tuition, and Mary's savings in order to repay the debt. Fred rides to Stone Court to tell Mary. She becomes distraught at what this will do to her parents financially. He, in turn, is distraught that Mary thinks he will never make anything of himself. After Fred leaves, Caleb arrives to tell Mary what has happened and to warn her against growing more fond of Fred than she already is.

Fred becomes ill; Wrench misdiagnoses this as a minor illness. At Rosamond's urging, Lydgate is called in for a second opinion. He realizes just how ill Fred is and treats him. Wrench does not take this kindly. While Lydgate is in attendance on Fred, Rosamond and the doctor become very well acquainted. He begins to spend his leisure time at the Vincys', earning enemies along the way for being Rosamond's favorite. Lydgate's being the Vincys' doctor leads other families to use his services. One of these is the Casaubons. The Brookes go there to welcome Dorothea and her husband home. During this visit, Celia announces to her sister that she will be marrying Chettam. He has proceeded with Dorothea's plans for the cottages.

Analysis

Fred seems self-destructive: first he fails his exams to avoid graduating and becoming a clergyman, then he learns to love hunting, riding, and billiards in his leisure time. The woman he loves will not marry him if he hypocritically becomes a clergyman, nor will she marry him if he is in debt and will not work. He cannot go to his father for money nor advice. His father has already lost a large sum of money on his education. Now he is alienating his friends, the Garths, by leaving them to repay the loan. He assured Caleb he could repay it himself if only Caleb would co-sign for him. Bambridge is not worried; he knows Fred or someone who believes in Fred will pay the debt. Fred is effectively turning away all those who believe in him: Mary, Caleb, Mrs. Garth, his father, even Featherstone. Only his mother still believes in him unconditionally, but the mores of the time demand she defer to her husband's wishes.

Study Questions

1. What does Diamond have to do with Fred repaying the loan?

2. Why does Mrs. Garth become so angry?

3. What is Mary's reaction to Fred's news?

4. What is Fred's purpose in declaring Mary will never have to speak to him again?

5. After Fred leaves, why does Caleb go to Stone Court?

6. What is Wrench's mistake when Fred becomes ill?

7. In what manner does Rosamond involve Lydgate in Fred's illness?

8. How do Rosamond and Lydgate become well acquainted?

9. Why isn't Mrs. Vincy watching out for her daughter's interests?

10. What were the circumstances under which Celia and Chettam become engaged?

Answers

1. In order to raise money to repay his debt, Fred was going to use his horse plus 30 pounds to buy Diamond, then sell him for the 80 pounds he was worth.

2. Mrs. Garth is so angry because she knew nothing of her husband's co-signing the loan. Now that Diamond has lamed himself, her family is going to have to repay Fred's loan.

3. Mary is distraught that Alfred's tuition and her parents' savings will have to be used to repay the debt. She professes not to be upset that her own savings will have to be used also.

4. Fred believes Mary thinks the worst of him and wants nothing to do with him. He loves her, so he intends to leave her alone.

5. Caleb wants to warn his daughter not to become too fond of Fred. He feels Fred's intentions are better than his actions.

6. Wrench sent medications instead of going to examine Fred, who was worse the next day. His mistake was in not going to see the patient before prescribing, and in not seeing the effect of the drugs.

7. Mrs. Vincy is crying for Sprague when Wrench is unavailable. Rosamond sees Lydgate outside their house and suggests that her mother call him in to tend to Fred.

8. Rosamond is left to herself a great deal during Fred's illness. Lydgate visits with her each time he comes to attend her brother.

9. Mrs. Vincy is so busy tending her favorite child during his bout with typhoid fever that she does not watch over her daughter as usual. She is with Fred all day, unless his father is home.

10. After Dorothea was married, Chettam continued to use the plan for her cottages on his property and to visit with the Brookes. Celia spent much time with him. She had no one else with whom to speak.

Suggested Essay Topics

1. Fred intends to make good his debt; however, he cannot. How does Fred's inability to repay the loan threaten the structure of Caleb's family?

2. Lydgate is successful in his treatment of his patients. Why, then, do the other doctors dislike him so?

Chapters 29–33

New Characters:

Mrs. Plymdale: *Ned's mother and Harriet Bulstrode's friend*

Trumbull: *an auctioneer and second cousin to Featherstone who takes a keen interest in Mary*

Summary

Dorothea is aiding her husband in his study. He gives her a letter from Ladislaw, which had been enclosed in a letter to him. They have harsh words before she even reads the letter. He ends the dispute by pleading the necessity of returning to his work. Dorothea also returns to her work, leaving the letter unread. Casaubon has some sort of attack and is in danger of fainting. Once he is resting comfortably, Chettam arrives and recommends they send for Lydgate. While happy in his marriage, Chettam still regrets that no one intervened when Dorothea planned to marry Casaubon. Lydgate orders Casaubon to find some relaxation or, at least, reduce the burden of his studies. Lydgate has a private meeting with Dorothea to tell her how important it is for Casaubon to moderate his work and avoid mental agitation if he is to live for many more years. Ladislaw has written to say he is on his way to England with the painting for which Casaubon sat. Dorothea gives the letter to her uncle, with instructions to tell Ladislaw that Casaubon can have no visitors now due to his illness. Brooke promises to do so, but his letter ends up including an invitation for Ladislaw to come to Tipton Grange.

Mrs. Vincy has accompanied Fred to Stone Court in order to keep him from Mary while he recuperates. Mrs. Bulstrode is told by Mrs. Plymdale that most people consider Lydgate and Rosamond engaged. She confronts her niece and warns her of Lydgate's poor financial standing, only to be told by Rosamond that she is wrong on both counts. Mrs. Bulstrode then confronts Lydgate, who tries to deflect her. He decides to stay away from the Vincys. When Lydgate attends Featherstone, Mrs. Vincy tells him to go to her house to fetch her husband. Featherstone is not doing well. Rosamond and he have an awkward reunion there, which

causes her to cry. He comforts her. He returns later that night to ask for her hand in marriage.

Featherstone's relatives have gathered at Stone Court. Only two are rich themselves—his brother, Solomon, and his sister, Jane. Mary is the intermediary between Featherstone and his family. He refuses to see any of them. The family is not kind to Mary, adding to her work and acting as if they think she steals from her uncle. While his relatives jockey for position in his will, Featherstone prefers the company of Fred and his mother. Trumbull keeps avoiding questions about the will. While Mary sits with her uncle that night, she worries that Fred will also be left out of the will. Featherstone directs her to get his iron chest, take out the two wills, and burn one of them. She refuses and he offers her money. When she still refuses, he tells her to fetch Fred. She refuses to do this also, offering to get the lawyer or fetch all the relatives. During the night, Featherstone dies.

Analysis

Mary is emerging as one of the most ethical characters in the novel. She gives her savings to her parents when they have need. She will not marry a hypocrite, nor an idler, nor one in debt. Mary will not touch any legal papers without witnesses, even—as she obviously suspects—if it will change the status of the man she loves from idler and debtor to debt-free and self-supporting. Despite her father's financial reversals and her mother's having to help support the family, Mary is not tempted to take Featherstone's money if it means doing something wrong. She cannot destroy a legal document in the hopes that doing so may benefit her love.

Dorothea, also, has her own strict code of ethics. She is married to a man she no longer admires, yet she denies herself in order to elongate his life. She enjoys Ladislaw's company, but knows Casaubon does not. Rather than risk the mental agitation Lydgate says her husband must avoid, she tells her uncle to write Ladislaw instructing him not to come to Lowick Manor. Of course, there is the question of why she did not write to Ladislaw herself.

The parallels between Mary and Dorothea are becoming apparent, despite the differences. Mary comes from the middle class. Her father, if he pays enough rent, will soon be granted the right to

vote under the new dictates of the Reform Act. Dorothea seems to have always had a family that owned enough land to vote, but was not of the "correct" religion to vote. Now her Protestant uncle will soon be eligible, and he is considering standing for Parliament. Once the Reform Act is passed, one will no longer need be Anglican to be a member of Parliament. Neither woman is willing to hurt another. Mary refuses to burn one of her uncle's wills. If she did so, someone would be out his or her inheritance, even though it might improve Fred's chances of inheriting. Dorothea will not harm her husband's health by having the company of Ladislaw, even if it means denying herself the warmth and life missing from her marriage.

Study Questions

1. About what do Dorothea and her husband argue?

2. In what way does Casaubon put a stop to the dispute?

3. For what reason are all his siblings at Featherstone's home?

4. In what manner do Featherstone's siblings treat Mary?

5. What is the purpose of Mrs. Vincy's presence at Stone Court?

6. How has it happened that Lydgate is Casaubon's physician?

7. In private, about what does Lydgate speak to Dorothea?

8. What request does Featherstone make of Mary?

9. What is Featherstone's objective in wanting his iron chest?

10. To what resolution does this last conflict between Mary and her uncle come?

Answers

1. Casaubon receives a letter from Ladislaw, with another letter in it to Dorothea. As he is giving this to her, Casaubon tells her in no uncertain terms he is not interested in having Ladislaw visit. Dorothea takes offense that her husband thinks she might want to do something annoying to him, such as this visit.

2. Casaubon pleads the need to get back to his work.

3. Featherstone's brothers and sisters, even the rich ones, are eager to make certain their names are in his will. He is dying, so this may be their last chance.

4. Most of Featherstone's relatives are unkind to Mary. They seem not to realize all the extra demands they make on her. Some of them seem to accuse her with their eyes of stealing from Featherstone.

5. Fred is convalescing at Stone Court. Now that he is stronger, his mother is more vigilant. She fears that he will fall into the clutches of the poorer Mary, whose mother actually gives lessons to earn an income.

6. Chettam comes in just after Casaubon's "attack" and firmly suggests that Dorothea send for Lydgate. He is still blaming himself for not intervening before she married Casaubon.

7. In private, Lydgate warns Dorothea that Casaubon must moderate his studies and avoid mental agitation if he is to live for many more years. He also tells her it is difficult to know how long Casaubon will live with this condition.

8. Featherstone wants Mary to fetch his iron chest and then his key while only the two of them are present.

9. Featherstone wants the iron chest because there are two wills in it. His plan is to have Mary burn one of them. He knows he will soon die.

10. This last conflict between Mary and Featherstone is not resolved. He dies when he had been alternately offering her money and railing at her to get the iron chest.

Suggested Essay Topics

1. Mary and Dorothea are two women from very different families, yet both are extremely ethical. Compare and contrast the possible sources of ethics for each of the women.

2. Casaubon appears to be very much adverse to his second cousin, Ladislaw. Trace this animosity from the first mention of it to the end of Book Three.

SECTION FIVE

Book Four:
Three Love Problems

Chapters 34–37

New Characters:

Rigg: *the person who will inherit most of Featherstone's possessions and Stone Court, if he adds the name "Featherstone" to his own name*

Sir Lydgate: *Lydgate's baronet uncle who Rosamond convinces Lydgate they must visit*

Summary

Featherstone is buried with a lavish funeral. Cadwallader presides. Dorothea, Mrs. Cadwallader, and the Chettams are at Lowick Manor, where they can watch the funeral train. Casaubon is working, having returned to his scholarly habits despite Lydgate's warnings that they must be moderated. Chettam remarks that most of the attendees are possible legatees, who have come from a distance, rather than neighbors. Brooke arrives to look in on Casaubon. They all discuss death in general, not noticing when Casaubon joins them. As they look out the window, Mrs. Cadwallader notices Rigg. Celia sees Ladislaw, which prompts Brooke to explain Ladislaw has been staying with him. Casaubon suspects Dorothea of asking her uncle to make that invitation. Brooke, unaware of this tension between his niece and her husband, fetches Ladislaw.

As Featherstone's relatives bicker among themselves and harbor their jealousy against the Vincys and Mary, the will is read. Standish had drawn up three wills, and fully expected to read the latest one. Featherstone had a fourth will drawn up by a different lawyer; this is the one Standish reads, including its codicil which had been added at an even later date. First, he reads the last will he'd written. Except for somewhat modest sums, personal bequests, and 10,000 pounds in vestments to Fred, all was left to Rigg, who only had to add the name Featherstone to his. The fourth will, the one which was a surprise, revoked most of the bequests and gave all the land within Lowick parish, the stock, and the household furniture to Rigg. The remaining land is to be used for Featherstone's Almshouses (poor houses), leaving those present at the reading—except Riggs and Trumbull, who inherited the gold-headed cane—with nothing. Fred thinks he must join the Church now.

Vincy wants Rosamond to wait until Lydgate has earned some money before they marry. He refuses to give them the money to set up housekeeping, and tells his wife to inform Rosamond of his decision. Rosamond ignores this. Mrs. Bulstrode asks her brother how he could allow Rosamond to become engaged when he knows nothing of Lydgate's family. He manages to turn this into a tirade against Mrs. Bulstrode's husband, who Vincy feels has not been kind toward Vincy's family. In an effort to speed the marriage date, Lydgate buys a house in Lowick Gate and orders all the necessary household items without thinking how he will pay for them. When Rosamond finally tells him what her father wants to do (although, by this time, Vincy is all for breaking the engagement entirely), Lydgate makes her promise to marry him within six weeks. Rosamond both wins over her father and cajoles Lydgate into arranging a visit with his uncle, Sir Lydgate, who is a baronet.

Much to the consternation of his neighbors, since Brooke's purchase of the *Pioneer* (a Middlemarch newspaper), he has employed Ladislaw as its editor. Casaubon no longer hides his dislike of Ladislaw. He dislikes his second cousin just as much, especially since the marriage to Dorothea. Ladislaw plans to waylay Dorothea when she is alone. Inclement weather forces him to take refuge at her home. The talk turns to Ladislaw's family. Finally, he asks her if she would object to his staying in Middlemarch to edit the *Pioneer*.

They agree he should do so. Dorothea asks Ladislaw to ask her husband's opinion. Ladislaw refuses and suggests she not mention this matter to her husband.

Upon Casaubon's arrival, Dorothea tells him of Ladislaw's visit and asks his opinion. He wants to know if Ladislaw had come to ask his opinion. Dorothea must say no. Casaubon writes a stern, cold letter to his second cousin. Ladislaw is no longer welcome at their home. Dorothea, knowing nothing of the letter, suggests to her husband that they share some of the wealth he has bestowed on her with Ladislaw, since he is family. Casaubon will not hear of it. Ladislaw writes a return letter to Casaubon thanking him for his past support but insisting it is not his affair where Ladislaw chooses to live. Casaubon is further insulted and thinks Ladislaw is interested in Dorothea. He endures his jealousy silently.

Analysis

Casaubon's jealousy grows as he realizes his own self-doubt. He has dutifully supported Ladislaw and his mother and is affronted, rather than pleased, when Ladislaw feels it is time to fend for himself. Ladislaw has not been disrespectful of either Casaubon or Dorothea, although he is well aware of his attraction to her.

Being headstrong, Casaubon ignores Lydgate's advice to curtail his scholarly endeavors. He needs to hide behind his books. Instead of explaining to his wife why he doesn't want Ladislaw in their home, he leads her to believe he thinks she is purposely attempting to displease him with Ladislaw's visits. But, as in Rome, she neither invited Ladislaw nor knew in advance of his visits. She makes no attempt to hide these visits from her husband. Why the jealousy? Is it possibly because he knows he is lacking in the kindness and affection a wife deserves? This jealousy, with which he suffers in silence, serves to further alienate Dorothea, working to his detriment.

Featherstone, in dying, did his own work promoting jealousy. The unexpected will made certain all his relatives would have nothing, including the Vincys and Mary. The relatives have just spent all the time Featherstone was dying being jealous of each other's assumed position in the will. They spent a great deal of energy being jealous of Mary—who they assumed was certain to be left at least a small inheritance, and the Vincys, particularly Fred, who they assumed would receive most of the inheritance. Whether or not this was Featherstone's intention, it was most effective. Mary refused to burn the latest will.

Force seems to be the key mode here, just as it would be in passing the Reform Act. Casaubon forces Dorothea to stop seeing Ladislaw by writing the letter. Rosamond forces Lydgate to marry her quickly by telling him of her father's desire they wait. Passage of the Reform Act was forced when King William IV had no choice but to reinstate the Whig Prime Minister Lord Grey. He took his recommendation to appoint 50 new peers to ensure the Act's passage. Revolution was threatened throughout the country after the third time the Act was rejected. The novel takes place before the passage of the Reform Act, but it was written after its passage.

Study Questions

1. Who is conducting Featherstone's funeral?

2. Which people have gathered at Lowick Gate?

3. Why has Brooke come there?

4. What are the provisions of the will Featherstone's lawyer thought he would be reading?

5. Why are these terms revoked?

6. What is Fred's reaction when the latest will is read?

7. What is Vincy's purpose in wanting Rosamond to wait to be married?

8. What is Lydgate doing while unaware of Vincy's decree?

9. What prompts Ladislaw to visit Dorothea?

10. In what manner does Casaubon respond to Ladislaw's latest visit?

Answers

1. Cadwallader is conducting Featherstone's funeral at Lowick. Featherstone disliked the other clergymen for various reasons.

2. Mrs. Cadwallader, Dorothea, and the Chettams (including Chettam's mother) have gathered at Lowick Manor. They can see the funeral train from the window.

3. Brooke says he has come to see about Casaubon's health. He also wants to say he invited Ladislaw to stay with him and will be offering him a job.

4. The provisions of the last will Featherstone's lawyer wrote are: small bequests to his relatives (including the Vincys but not Mary), Fred to have 10,000 pounds in specified investments, and all else to Rigg when he takes the name Featherstone.

5. The unexpected will leaves Rigg, providing he take the name Featherstone, with the property in Lowick proper, the stock, and the household furniture. Except for some small bequests, including the gold-headed cane to Trumbull, all else was to be used for the Featherstone Alms-houses.

6. When this latest will is read, Fred declares he must pass his exams and join the Church now.

7. Vincy had fully expected Fred to inherit. Vincy still has to pay for the schooling Fred never finished. He thinks Lydgate expects to be established with Rosamond in their new home. He vows he will not do this. They had better wait until they have their own money.

8. Lydgate, unaware of Vincy's decision, is spending money he has not yet earned, preparing a home. While he did not necessarily expect Vincy to do this for them, he is not considering the amount he is spending.

9. Ladislaw visits Dorothea because he longs to talk with her again as they did in Rome. He tells her it is because her uncle has offered him the editorship of the *Pioneer* and he wonders if she would object to his staying in the area.

10. Casaubon is jealous of his second cousin's time with Dorothea and insulted that Ladislaw has not asked his opinion as to whether to stay in the area or not. He writes a scathing letter informing Ladislaw he is no longer welcome in their home.

Suggested Essay Topics

1. The Vincys and the Garths are both relatives of Featherstone's and are kind to him in his illness. Why do Featherstone's other relatives resent them?

2. Dorothea seems unaware that Casaubon is jealous of Ladislaw, yet she unwittingly feeds this jealousy. In what ways does she do this?

Chapters 38–42

New Characters:

Dagley: *one of Brooke's tenants whose son has been found poaching and who insults Brooke*

Raffles: *Rigg's estranged stepfather*

Summary

Brooke is thinking of becoming a candidate for Parliament. He has made Ladislaw the editor of the *Pioneer*, which upsets the Cadwalladers and Chettams. Chettam wants Brooke to ask Caleb, who Brooke dismissed 12 years ago, to return to the management of his property. Chettam will also ask Caleb to manage his estates. When Brooke arrives unexpectedly, Cadwallader gives him a copy of the *Trumpet* in which Brooke is attacked. Mrs. Cadwallader tries to dissuade Brooke by bringing up the expense of being a candidate, since it is known that Brooke is tight-fisted. Chettam attempts to explain that Brooke has people in his party who will harm his chances at election.

As they each take turns arguing against Brooke's methods of landlording, he parries them and insists on the public life they are trying to avoid for him. They are worried that he will be crucified by the press for the poor condition in which he keeps his tenants' cottages. Chettam plots to gain Dorothea's influence over her uncle; she is to speak as if Brooke had already decided to have repairs made and the cottages improved. When Brooke defers, she explains this is a good plan for one who wants to be elected on a platform

of Improvement of the people. Ladislaw watches in admiration as she speaks to her uncle. They are interrupted by a footman who announces one of Dagley's sons has been found poaching.

While Brooke goes to attend to the problem, Ladislaw and Dorothea remain behind. He tells her Casaubon has forbidden his presence at their home and asks if she had known this. She feels terrible but cannot speak against her husband. This means they will almost never see each other. Brooke must go to the Dagleys, so he leaves with his niece. As he arrives at the Dagleys, he realizes how very dismal the cottage is. A drunken Dagley refuses to punish his son, which causes Brooke to go to Mrs. Dagley. This infuriates Dagley, who rages at Brooke about being a bad landlord. He is confused; he'd thought the tenants were pleased when he took over the management of his own land from Caleb 12 years earlier.

Caleb receives the letter from Chettam asking him to manage the Chettam estates and Brooke's Tipton property, which saves Mary from having to accept a position she was not eager to have. Farebrother arrives as Fred's envoy to tell the Garths that Fred has gone to study for his degree again. He doesn't know what it is he wants to do with it. He couldn't come himself to say good-bye to them because he is so miserable about not being able to repay the debt himself. Caleb tells Farebrother about Mary's refusal to burn the latest will for Featherstone, but cautions him to keep this secret. Farebrother rejects his own regard for Mary. Caleb tells his wife that if Fred will not be a parson, he would like to teach him estate management. She convinces him to wait until Fred finishes school to see if he knows then what he wants to do. Caleb mentions that both Rigg and Bulstrode had come to him for assessments on the value of Stone Court. Raffles arrives at Stone Court and attempts to cajole money from Riggs, who refuses and wants never to see Raffles again. Before Raffles leaves, Riggs gives him brandy and a coin. While he is getting them, Raffles sees a scrap of paper and uses it to make his flask firmer within its leather casing. The paper had Bulstrode's name on it, but Raffles did not know that.

Casaubon is suffering, thinking that Dorothea is critical, not loving. Ladislaw is filling her with new, objectional ideas. Dorothea does not mention her last visit with him to her husband. Casaubon asks Lydgate to give him his opinion about his health and expected life span before adding a codicil to his will affecting Dorothea's possibility of marrying Ladislaw. He sees this as a way of protecting his future widow from a young man who wants to take advantage of a rich, young widow. Lydgate tells him he has heart disease. With care, he may live another 15 years, but sudden death would not be unusual. He also confirms he has told Dorothea part of the diagnosis. Dorothea comes out to find her husband after Lydgate leaves, and leads him into the house. He isolates himself in the library. They each prefer to dine alone and meet again in bed.

Analysis

We already know that Featherstone was married first to Caleb's sister (which makes Mary his niece), then to Vincy's wife's sister (which makes Fred and Rosamond his nephew and niece). Not only is he the link between the Garths and the Vincys, but Rigg appears to be his illegitimate child whose stepfather is Raffles. The Vincy and Garth children grew up running in and out of each others' homes. It is only Caleb's financial reversals which caused the breach between the adults. Mrs. Vincy now looks down upon the poorer Garths, ignoring her own husband's recent financial reversals. Fred still feels very comfortable with these same adults, comfortable enough to go to his "almost" uncle to ask him to co-sign a loan instead of going to his father. Fred and Mary are fond of each other, but she is well aware of her "almost" aunt's aversion to having Fred marry her when she is poor and her "aunt's" delusions that Mary is trying to snag Fred for his money. Rigg is something of a surprise, having neither been raised locally nor introduced to the others. His mother has been kept a secret (as has his existence), but his inheritance brings his estranged stepfather to Stone Court. It is almost as if the reader could see a genealogical chart of the family ties.

The interweavings among the families mirror those among the political parties. Whigs were opposed to the ruling Tory party. The two parties were polarized by the religious issues of the Reform Act. Both felt the bill to be radical. By the late 1820s, the Tories lost office. It was the Whigs who were considered the liberals. By 1834, the Tories agreed to work within the reforms. The Radicals felt the bill was the first step in reform, but also wanted its passage. We may see here some sort of genealogy of the changes the Reform Act "birthed" in the British government.

Study Questions

1. What is Brooke planning to do?
2. Why are Chettam and the Cadwalladers opposed to this plan?
3. What proposal does Chettam bring to Brooke?
4. What attempts does Chettam make to convince Brooke to do as he wants?
5. About what does Ladislaw speak to Dorothea?
6. For what reason does Brooke leave with Dorothea?
7. In what manner does Dagley treat Brooke?
8. How is Mary saved from taking a position of which she is not fond?
9. What is Farebrother's message to the Garths from Fred?
10. For what purpose has Raffles come to Stone Court?

Answers

1. Brooke has decided to stand for Parliament and is using the *Pioneer*, under Ladislaw's editorship, as his political voice.
2. Chettam and the Cadwalladers are opposed to Brooke's plan. He is being publicly denounced, through the *Trumpet*, as a poor landlord. They fear he doesn't realize he is exposing his private life to public scrutiny.
3. Chettam proposes that Brooke rehire Caleb, who was dismissed 12 years ago, to manage Tipton. Chettam will also hire Caleb to manage his estates.
4. Chettam has Dorothea visit Brooke and speak as if it were a foregone conclusion that he will repair and improve the cottages he rents to his tenants.
5. Ladislaw tells Dorothea that Casaubon has written him a letter saying Ladislaw is no longer welcome in their home.

6. Brooke leaves with Dorothea to see Dagley, one of his tenants whose son has been caught poaching.

7. Dagley insults Brooke and denounces him as a bad landlord who should not be managing his own cottages.

8. A letter arrives from Chettam offering Caleb the management of both Tipton and Chettam's estates. This will afford an income such that Mary will not have to add an income for the family, which frees her from taking the position she really didn't like.

9. Fred sends Farebrother to the Garths to tell them he has gone back to school and is too miserable at being unable to repay the debt to come in person to say good-bye.

10. Raffles comes to Stone Court because he wants to cajole money from his estranged stepson now that Riggs has inherited Featherstone's property.

Suggested Essay Topics

1. Brooke is confused that he is thought to be a bad landlord by Dagley. Considering that he will be standing for Parliament on a platform of making improvements for the people, how are Dorothea, Chettam, and the Cadwalladers right in thinking he should not run for office?

2. Caleb is eager to offer Fred a position, but Mrs. Garth thinks it more prudent to wait until he finishes school and decides what he'd like to do with his life. Which position would you take and why?

Book Five:
The Dead Hand

Chapters 43–47

New Character:

Nancy Nash: *the patient misdiagnosed by another doctor and successfully treated by Lydgate*

Summary

Dorothea calls at Lydgate's and finds Ladislaw and Rosamond; Lydgate is at the hospital. Ladislaw is mortified to be found alone with another woman, not realizing Rosamond sees he adores Dorothea. Dorothea wonders why Rosamond entertains another man when her husband is not home. While Dorothea is with Lydgate at the hospital, asking if there is any change in her husband's condition, she agrees to donate handsomely to the new hospital. He tells her of the opposition in the town to helping the hospital because of the dislike for Bulstrode. By telling Casaubon she'd been to see Lydgate, Dorothea unwittingly widens the gap between them. He now feels her affection for him is only because he may die. Lydgate manages to weaken his position. He has aligned himself with Bulstrode and follows new medical practices. The other doctors feel they know more than Lydgate and are suspicious of his medical opinions. Luckily for Lydgate, he is having success with his methods, especially with Nancy Nash and Trumbull, which saves his reputation and his practice.

Nonetheless, once Bulstrode appoints Lydgate as the chief medical superintendent, the other medical practitioners refuse to join the hospital. Lydgate is undaunted. Bulstrode vows to work all the harder to raise the money necessary for the building and staff Lydgate wants. Farebrother cautions Lydgate to separate himself from Bulstrode as much as possible and to stay clear of debt in order to protect himself from the malicious feud which is brewing. Rosamond begins to regret that Lydgate is a medical man, thinking he has lowered his position in becoming one.

Ladislaw and Brooke continue Brooke's campaign for Parliament through the *Pioneer*. Ladislaw, too, suffers from gossip, which says Casaubon will have nothing to do with him. Politics leads him to the homes of those in favor of Reform. He spends a great deal of time with little children, Miss Noble, and the Lydgates. Lydgate agrees that Brooke is not made to be a public man. Lydgate and Ladislaw have an animated dispute about whether or not it is necessary to have an "immaculate man" before trying for reform. Rosamond puts an end to this. Rosamond is pregnant, and Lydgate withholds the information from her that there is a bill he cannot pay. Missing Dorothea terribly, Ladislaw goes to church knowing she will be there. He is surprised by his discomfort at seeing her when she arrives. When her husband arrives, he is almost paralyzed. He sees it was stupid to think it might have been amusing to vex Casaubon by appearing in church.

Analysis

Misunderstandings abound as the new hospital is being developed. Bulstrode, no favorite of the townspeople, is repulsing people left and right with his decrees as to how the hospital will be run. He feels he has the right to do this as the chief financial source, but has no insight into the politics involved with this position. Lydgate is already under suspicion simply because the unpopular Bulstrode is the one who brought him to Middlemarch. Adding to his unpopularity is the new way he practices medicine, and, more importantly, his lack of political awareness. While he does not steal patients nor "bad mouth" the other, older doctors already established in their practices, he is quick to give his opinion without thinking about the ramifications of whatever it is he says. He does not seek out the older men to explain, and he doesn't soothe their injured feelings. He is an innocent when it comes to social or business politics.

Ladislaw is very much like Lydgate in this instance. He also does not seem to realize that by estranging Casaubon and aligning himself with Brooke, the unpopular candidate for Parliament and a man who is commonly accepted as a poor landlord, he is putting himself in an awkward position. Both men are new to the area and have not taken the time to establish themselves before making their opinions vehemently and widely known. Both men seem unaware of the damage they may be doing to their reputations, although Farebrother does try to gently advise Lydgate.

Bulstrode seems to be representative of the aristocracy. He is monied, a landowner, presumably of the correct religion, and expects to have his decrees followed without question. While he may consider himself a benevolent being, as does the aristocratic Anglican Parliament, he is now being questioned. The townspeople are voicing their dislike of him. Similarly, prior to the Reform Act's passage, farm laborers rioted in the southeast of England and there was unrest in the manufacturing districts.

Study Questions

1. What does Dorothea's asking Lydgate about her husband's condition further weakens her marriage?

2. Why is Ladislaw distressed that Dorothea finds him visiting with Rosamond?

3. What request does Lydgate make of Dorothea?

4. What is the local opinion of the new doctor?

5. How is Bulstrode harming Lydgate's progress in Middlemarch?

6. Farebrother offers Lydgate what advice?

7. Ladislaw decides he must take what course of action?

8. Why isn't Ladislaw readily accepted in his new home?

9. How does Ladislaw spend his time?

10. Why does Lydgate withhold information from Rosamond?

Answers

1. Casaubon suffers not only from heart disease, but also from self-doubt. He already feels his wife is attracted to Ladislaw's personality. Casaubon now suspects she shows affection for him only because he may die at any time.

2. Lydgate is at the hospital when Dorothea goes to his home to seek information about her husband's condition. Rosamond and Ladislaw are alone. Ladislaw is afraid the woman he worships, Dorothea, will think the less of him for being entertained by another woman without the proper chaperon present.

3. Lydgate explains the financial difficulties in starting the new hospital and asks for Dorothea's support. She readily agrees to donate 200 pounds a year.

4. People are suspicious of Lydgate: he is new to the area; his mentor at the new hospital is the much disliked Bulstrode; and he has brought with him from Paris new and strange medical practices.

5. Bulstrode is disliked because he is a zealously religious man, tends to be lordly and overbearing, is involved with trade, and—most importantly—has brought in an outsider (Lydgate) to be the chief medical superintendent of the new hospital.

6. Farebrother kindly warns Lydgate to distance himself as much as possible from Bulstrode so as not to fall under the shadow of the town's dislike for him.

7. Ladislaw is quietly suffering from wanting to see Dorothea. Knowing he cannot see her alone, he resolves to go to church when she will be there. He not only will have the chance to see her there, but he might succeed in vexing Casaubon by his appearance.

8. Ladislaw is not accepted because he is new to the area; few know anything about his family or background; he is aligned with Brooke in politics; and the rumor is that his second cousin wants nothing to do with him.

9. When not giving fiery speeches in favor of Reform on behalf of his benefactor, Brooke, or working as the editor of Brooke's paper, he visits with Miss Noble or leads the children on expeditions, as well as visiting with both the Lydgates.

10. Rosamond is pregnant. Lydgate does not want her to worry that there is a bill he cannot pay. He does not tell her.

Suggested Essay Topics

1. Lydgate is beginning to realize his position in Middlemarch. How has he arrived at such a dismal point in so short a time?

2. Ladislaw and Lydgate have become friends rather quickly. How do you account for this friendship?

Chapters 48–53

New Character:

Sarah Dunkirk Ladislaw: *Ladislaw's mother and Bulstrode's secret stepdaughter*

Summary

Dorothea realizes she cannot please her husband. He has reversed his aversion to having her work with him. Casaubon asks his wife to work with him after dinner. Later, in bed, she reads to him as usual. He complains of discomfort and asks if she will follow his wishes for her should he die. Dorothea pleads to think this over at least until morning. They meet in the library the next morning. She tells him she will join him in the garden with her answer. She can't answer him; he has died in the garden while awaiting her decision. Lydgate is then called to attend her since she has become delirious. Dorothea is still confined to bed the day after Casaubon's funeral. Chettam and Brooke discover the codicil to Casaubon's will, directing her never to marry Ladislaw on consequence of losing all her inheritance from her husband. Chettam pleads with Brooke to send Ladislaw away and save Dorothea from any more pain. Brooke insists she is an adult and will do as she pleases.

After a period of recuperation at Celia's, Dorothea is eager to return to Lowick Manor and resume her husband's affairs, much to the consternation of her uncle. Celia tells her sister of Casaubon's codicil to the will, which serves to shock Dorothea into realizing the revulsion she holds for Casaubon and the fondness she feels for Ladislaw. Lydgate agrees Dorothea may return home if that is going to give her the most peace of mind.

Once home, but only for a visit, she searches everywhere for some private writing of Casaubon's but finds nothing. She wants to speak to Lydgate about Tyke's being appointed the chaplain for the new hospital, but he introduces Farebrother as a better choice. Lydgate casually mentions Ladislaw in their conversation. Ladislaw, avoiding the Grange where he might run into Dorothea, busy with the *Pioneer* and Brooke's candidacy, knows nothing of the codicil. Brooke has too much sherry before giving a speech and makes a fool of himself, which results in his being pelted with raw eggs. Ladislaw resolves to leave for five years and earn his living at writing and giving of speeches and make his mark in the world. But not yet—not until Dorothea knows why he will not suggest marriage to her. Brooke unexpectedly suggests Ladislaw move on.

Having taken the post at Lowick (although keeping the post at St. Botolph's), Farebrother and Miss Noble are rejoicing in their good fortune. Miss Noble innocently tells Farebrother she wishes he would marry Mary. Fred returns from school and asks Farebrother if he had been able to convince Vincy that the clergy is not for Fred. When told no, Fred wonders what he can do now except go into the church. He loves Mary and cannot earn any money for them in any other way. Mary has already said she will not marry him if he hypocritically enters the church. He wants Farebrother to find out from Mary if she still will not marry him should he become a clergyman. When he sees her, Mary tells Farebrother she will not commit to marrying Fred. She certainly would never marry Fred if he were clergy. When he tells her she must be certain not to think of harboring another love while Fred is becoming worthy, Mary gets the strangest impression that he may be this love of which he speaks. She agrees she cares for Fred too much to love another. Farebrother reassures Mary she acted properly in refusing to get the iron chest and burn the latest will for Featherstone.

Bulstrode purchases Stone Court not more than 15 months after Featherstone's death and bequest of Stone Court to Rigg, approximately the same time Farebrother assumes the Vicarage at Lowick Manor. As Bulstrode confers with Caleb, Raffles appears, thinking Rigg still owns Stone Court. He wants to obtain Bulstrode's current address from him. Raffles hasn't seen Bulstrode in 25 years. Caleb is uncomfortable and leaves. Bulstrode is clearly displeased at seeing Raffles and attempts to rid himself of this unwanted visitor by inviting him to stay at Stone Court overnight while he returns to The Shrubs. The next day, Raffles reveals he has returned from ten years in America, widowed, and not wanting to work. Bulstrode agrees to pay blackmail. Raffles must keep his distance and not tell that he had found the daughter of Bulstrode's first wife before their marriage. Bulstrode suppressed that information in order to inherit the somewhat questionable, but profitable, family business upon his marriage. Raffles tells of his own marriage, never mentioning his stepson may have been Featherstone's illegitimate child. He does, however, strengthen his blackmail case by saying he has the last name of Bulstrode's first wife's daughter somewhere. Alone, he searches his mind for the name and remembers it is Ladislaw. He has no intention of telling Bulstrode.

Analysis

The plot and family connections become even more intricate. We already know of the connections between the Vincys and Garths via Featherstone. It has also been mentioned that Bulstrode is Vincy's brother-in-law via Vincy's sister, Mrs. Bulstrode, who is married to Bulstrode. We suspect that Rigg is Featherstone's illegitimate son. Why else would the old man have left him most of his property and ordered him to add "Featherstone" to his name? We already know that Raffles is Rigg's estranged stepfather. Now we discover that Raffles worked for Bulstrode 25 years ago, trying to find the daughter of the woman Bulstrode wanted to marry so that the daughter could inherit her father's lucrative business before her mother remarried and gave it to Bulstrode. We also discover that woman's married name was Ladislaw. Ladislaw is a man new to Middlemarch. All that is known about him is that his grandmother (Casaubon's aunt) made an unfortunate marriage. Was this the marriage to the first husband who built up the very shady, but very lucrative business from which Ladislaw's mother ran away to be on the stage?

Fred chooses his friend, Farebrother, to be his emissary to his love, Mary, only to have her suspect Farebrother is in love with her himself. Rosamond entertains Ladislaw, Dorothea finds him alone with her, and Ladislaw feels he is ruined in Dorothea's eyes. The interweaving between the families and the mistaken actions among the friends almost gives the reader the feeling that the characters are strangling each other emotionally.

Once again, this "strangulation" may be taken as a reflection of the times, politically. Lord Grey, the Prime Minister, symbolically had to strangle King William IV by resigning when the Reform Act was apparently going to be defeated for the third time. When the Duke of Wellington was made Grey's successor, the threat of revolution became very real. The king had no choice but to reinstate Grey and appoint the 50 new peers he had suggested in order to be certain there would be enough pro votes to pass the bill. George Eliot knew this, although it hadn't taken place yet during the setting of her novel.

Study Questions

1. What is Casaubon's usual method of having his wife work with him?

2. What are the circumstances of Casaubon's death?

3. Casaubon adds what codicil to his will?

4. What warning did Dorothea have of this codicil?

5. For what reason does Ladislaw think he should leave Middlemarch?

6. What is Brooke's motive in resisting the idea of sending Ladislaw away?

7. What is the purpose in Farebrother's going to see Mary?

8. Of what is it that Mary has a fleeting impression?

9. Why is Bulstrode at Stone Court?

10. What astounding information do we know of Bulstrode's past?

Answers

1. Casaubon has Dorothea do the necessary writing in the library, then she reads to him in bed as he selects information for his books.

2. Casaubon dies the day after complaining of discomfort while trying to sleep. He'd gone for a walk in the garden, sat on a bench, and simply expired.

3. Casaubon adds the codicil that Dorothea would lose her sizable inheritance from him if she marries Ladislaw.

4. The night before his death, Casaubon had asked Dorothea to promise to carry out the terms of his will. He refused to tell her what the terms are.

5. Ladislaw resolves to leave Middlemarch for five years to make his mark upon the world with his writing and speaking, but not until Dorothea knows why he is leaving. He feels he cannot come to her empty-handed because she is a wealthy widow.

6. Brooke feels Dorothea has always been an independent, headstrong young girl who knows her own mind. Now that she is of legal age, nothing will deter her from her chosen course. He also feels Ladislaw is doing a wonderful job of helping to get him elected and is not so eager to lose his confidential secretary.

7. Fred has finished college and is thinking of joining the clergy, but is worried Mary will not marry him if he does. He sends his friend, Farebrother, to find out if this is so.

8. Farebrother explains to Mary that if she will not marry Fred until he has proven himself worthy, she must not love someone else until she has given Fred the time to prove himself worthy. She gets the impression Farebrother is pleading his own case as the someone else who wonders if there is a chance for him.

9. Bulstrode is there with Caleb to see about some repairs before moving there.

10. The reader discovers that Bulstrode had cheated the young woman who was his stepdaughter through his first marriage by suppressing her whereabouts. His wife had wanted to give her daughter the opportunity to inherit the family business before it was given to the new husband.

Suggested Essay Topics

1. The townspeople are having a feud with Bulstrode, saying he is, among other things, too ostentatiously religious and masterful. Now we learn he has cheated his stepdaughter of her inheritance. How can we explain his present personality in terms of his previous actions?

2. Explain in detail, using facts from the novel, why you think Ladislaw may or may not suspect his relationship with Bulstrode.

Book Six: The Widow and His Wife

Chapters 54–58

New Character:

Captain Lydgate: *the third son of Lydgate's baronet uncle, Sir Lydgate*

Summary

Celia is enthralled with her baby, Arthur, but Dorothea finds she needs to do more than watch his every movement. After three months at Freshitt Hall, she returns permanently to Lowick Manor. Dorothea refuses to accept a companion there. She makes her private peace with her deceased husband and catches glimpses of Ladislaw whenever she can. Ladislaw surprises her by arriving to announce he will be leaving Middlemarch; he is chagrined that she is not disappointed. Misunderstanding his distress, she offers him the miniature of his grandmother. He is perplexed and declares it is not going to add to his possessions, which for the first time, he regrets are so meager. As he battles with himself as to whether or not she loves him, Chettam arrives. This prompts Ladislaw to take his leave. At a later dinner held at Freshitt Hall, Chettam, Dorothea, Mrs. Cadwallader, and Chettam's mother discuss remarriage before the end of the year of mourning for the first husband. Dorothea insists this has nothing to do with her. She intends never to marry again.

Dorothea hires Caleb whenever there is work to do with the tenements or farms attached to her home. The railway was to lay a line through Lowick parish. As Caleb is on his way to sell part of Lowick parish to the railway, he sees some laborers threatening several railway workers. Fred, who happens to ride by, sees Caleb and his assistant go to the aid of the railway people. Caleb's young assistant is knocked unconscious. He enters into the fray driving off the laborers. Caleb will lose a day's work. His assistant has painfully sprained his ankle. Fred offers to do his job. Caleb explains to the laborers that the railway is inevitable. It will not do to keep fighting its workers, who are just doing their jobs as are the laborers.

Fred asks Caleb if he may work for him and marry Mary. Caleb, ever conscious of his wife's feelings, asks Fred to let him consider this overnight. She does object, informing her husband that Farebrother is also fond of Mary. Caleb insists it is Fred whom Mary loves. He will offer Fred a job to make it easier for Mary. Vincy is greatly disappointed that this is what Fred chooses to do with his life. Except for being allowed to live at home, Fred is cut off as far as money is concerned. Mrs. Vincy is disappointed he will be marrying Mary. This, on top of learning Rosamond has lost her baby. Fred goes to Mrs. Garth. She thinks, although Mary is unaware of it, that Farebrother is fond of Mary. Fred is surprised and wonders if Mrs. Garth thinks he is standing in their way. He goes to the parsonage—where Farebrother manages to get them time alone—and asks Mary, who promptly tells him she loves no other.

Rosamond's baby was born prematurely when she went riding with Lydgate's cousin. Her husband had warned her this was not safe. Lydgate is in debt and still hiding it from his wife. He arrives home determined to tell her, but Ladislaw is there. Sensing Lydgate needs to speak to his wife alone, he bids them good-night. When Lydgate explains the debt to Rosamond and the need to sell some of their possessions to meet the bills, she feels she cannot do anything to help. She is surprised he has not asked her father to help. He refuses to do so, and will not allow her to do so. She wants to know why they cannot simply move away. He refuses again, trying to explain they must have money to do that and also trying to involve her in the business of solving their debt. She wants no part of it and tells him she will be at her father's the next day. He convinces her not to leave the inventory to the servants, but to be home to help. He realizes she will not take kindly to the discussion they must soon have about their future finances.

Analysis

While Fred is solidifying his future, Rosamond is letting hers slip out of her grasp. Fred has finished college as he promised his father he would and found the courage to tell his father he will not be going into the clergy. Accidentally, he has found employment at which he is willing to work hard and learn, and has an employer for whom he already has regard and respect.

He faces Mrs. Garth to tell her he would like to marry Mary and confronts Mary directly when Mrs. Garth suggests that Farebrother is his rival for Mary's affections. He goes to Farebrother's home when he is not certain whether Farebrother is a rival or the friend he feels Farebrother is.

His sister, on the other hand, has lost her first baby via a premature birth due to riding an untried horse. Her husband/doctor told her it was dangerous. It was more important to her to have the neighbors see her riding with the son of a baronet (Sir Lydgate's son and Lydgate's cousin). She is still denying the ride was the cause of the baby's death and now, when her husband is in financial trouble, she also denies she can help him. Emotionally, she will not join him in the job of making good on the debt; she even wants to be gone when the inventory people come to see what their furniture may be worth. She becomes cold when he tries to explain that the jewelry and some other items will have to be returned. She is shutting down and shutting him out.

It's not surprising that the laborers became enraged at the railway workers. The railway (as it is called in England) was a source of contention for many people at this time. Originally built for only short trips to carry coal privately, the first public railroad line to carry other goods had been introduced only several years earlier in 1825. Although it did introduce new jobs, the railway was usually thought of as a monster traveling at the unheard of and noisy speed of 35 miles an hour, spewing smoke from its engine as it went.

Study Questions

1. What motive does Dorothea have in rejecting the suggestion to have a companion once she returns to Lowick Manor?

2. Why isn't Dorothea disturbed by the discussion about remarriage before the end of the year of a widow's mourning?

3. For what reason is Caleb at the site of the fracas?

4. How is it that Fred happens to be nearby when the farm laborers threaten the railway workers?

5. For what does Fred ask Caleb?

6. What are Mrs. Garth's initial objections?

7. What is Fred's purpose in going to the parsonage?

8. In what manner did Rosamond lose her baby?

9. After Ladislaw leaves, what news does Lydgate give his wife?

10. What response does this news elicit from Rosamond?

Answers

1. Dorothea wants no companion because she wants to be alone at Lowick Manor, to make her peace with her deceased husband and to see Ladislaw.

2. Dorothea takes no offense at the discussion of remarriage before the end of a year of mourning because she plans never to marry again.

3. Caleb has been hired by Dorothea and is on his way to meet some railway people to sell some of her land to them.

4. Vincy sent his son riding on this fine day. Fred was just deciding which way to go when he saw Caleb and the fracas.

5. Fred wants Caleb to hire him permanently and teach him the profession so that he may be an honorable man.

6. Mrs. Garth thinks Farebrother is interested in Mary and would be a better choice as her husband. She also believes Fred wrong in not seeing this and using Farebrother as his emissary to assure himself of Mary's love.

7. Fred goes to the parsonage to find Mary and see if she prefers Farebrother.

8. Rosamond lost her baby by going riding with Captain Lydgate, at his request and against her husband's advice, on the untried horse.

9. Once Ladislaw leaves, Lydgate tells his wife they are in debt and must sell some of their things.

10. Rosamond thinks she must ask her father for money. Lydgate has not. Then she thinks moving away to London will be the answer to their financial problems. She is barely acquiescent when he tries to make amends between them with a kiss.

Suggested Essay Topics

1. Ladislaw has not minded being poor before. What is it that changes his feelings about his financial position now?

2. Dorothea neither desires to remarry nor court Ladislaw, yet her feelings are beginning to overcome her resolutions. How is this illustrated in the text?

Chapters 59–62

Summary

Rosamond tells Ladislaw not to go to London. Dorothea likes him far more than her fortune. When he demands to know what she is talking about, Rosamond tells Ladislaw about the codicil. He leaves, astonished, declaring he will never marry Dorothea. Unbeknownst to Lydgate, Rosamond has gone to her father for financial aid and been refused. An auction is held locally, to which Trumbull invites Ladislaw. Raffles accosts Ladislaw, asking if his mother was Sarah Dunkirk. Startled, Ladislaw challenges Raffles, who only asks if his parents are still alive.

During an unplanned encounter that evening, Raffles talks of when Ladislaw was small, how much he resembles his father, and wonders aloud why his mother ran away. He makes certain to refer to the "respectable thieving line" that Sarah's father was in. When they part, Ladislaw feels sullied.

Bulstrode returns home only to have his wife tell him an unagreeable sort was asking for him. The following day, Raffles sees Bulstrode at the bank. He will stay in Middlemarch as long as he chooses. He expects more money from Bulstrode, who by now is terrified Raffles will tell all. His wife knows only that he had married a dissenter. Bulstrode asks Ladislaw to come see him. During their meeting, Bulstrode asks Ladislaw to verify his parentage. Bulstrode explains he married Ladislaw's grandmother. Ladislaw is entitled to share Bulstrode's wealth, part of which would have gone to Sarah Dunkirk, had she been found. Ladislaw answers that Bulstrode did know of Sarah's whereabouts. Bulstrode does not deny this but proceeds to negotiate. Ladislaw wants to know if Bulstrode was involved in the family business and if it was that of thieves and convicts. He then refuses the money, since it is more important to him to keep his honor, and leaves.

Ladislaw can now think only of seeing Dorothea again and leaving Middlemarch. He is unaware of her private income, and thinks marrying him will leave her penniless. Mrs. Cadwallader is called in by Chettam to warn Dorothea away from Ladislaw. Dorothea calls her reports of Ladislaw's approaching Rosamond false. She defends his honor but privately has her own doubts. She flees to Tipton only to find Ladislaw in her uncle's library. He tells her he had written to her at Lowick Manor, asking to see her once more before he leaves. This time, he has no intention of coming back. He speaks of having to do without happiness, and she thinks he is referring to Rosamond. As he leaves, she realizes it is she he loves. She is in the carriage and overtakes him as she drives; she cannot bring herself to stop the carriage.

Analysis

The Middlemarchers' inability to speak plainly is causing all kinds of misunderstandings among them. Ladislaw, horrified at Casaubon's codicil, thinks he will be leaving Dorothea penniless if he marries her. Had he only spoken with her, he would have known of her private income and not felt he had to leave Middlemarch and his love forever. Dorothea, for her part, is not certain to whom Ladislaw refers when he laments the love he can never have. Rosamond is married, and to Ladislaw's friend at that; he does spend an inordinate amount of time with her when her husband is not present. Wouldn't that cause him to flee the situation rather than bring pain to his friend? Bulstrode did not tell his present wife the full circumstances of his former marriage and now fears exposure. Instead of presenting the circumstances to Ladislaw plainly, he hedges, offering a financial settlement which affronts Ladislaw's honor. Raffles hints, hints, hints: to Bulstrode about what he may or may not do; to Ladislaw about his parents; and to Mrs. Bulstrode simply by appearing at The Shrubs asking for Bulstrode. Even Chettam is not speaking plainly, preferring to have Mrs. Cadwallader present Ladislaw's worst traits in an attempt to make Dorothea reject him. Miss Noble speaks plainly but is not taken seriously.

The Middlemarchers' provinciality seems to be making them miserable. Had Dorothea not been so shocked to see Ladislaw's hands on Rosamond's face, she could have asked each of them some questions. Bulstrode may be less provincial than the others, but his wife has a hard time living with the fact that her husband's first wife was a dissenter. Now she learns information that goes against the grain of all the rigid rules of their small society. Ladislaw, despite his having traveled, easily lapses into the provinciality he'd supposedly outgrown with his art and traveling and is convinced he cannot marry Dorothea.

Study Questions

1. What has happened to the siblings?

2. Why does Lydgate tell Rosamond not to mention the codicil to Ladislaw?

3. For what reason does Rosamond tell Ladislaw about the codicil?

4. What are the circumstances under which Ladislaw and Raffles meet?

5. About what does Raffles question Ladislaw?

6. What is the purpose in Raffles seeking Bulstrode?

7. What is Bulstrode's motive in sending for Ladislaw?

8. What response does Ladislaw have to Bulstrode's proposition?

9. Why does Ladislaw want to see Dorothea?

10. How do Ladislaw and Dorothea accidentally meet?

Answers

1. There is a distance between the siblings since Fred announced his engagement to Mary and gave up all thoughts of entering the clergy.

2. Lydgate knows Ladislaw cares for Dorothea. That would make this codicil even more painful to Ladislaw. He cautions Rosamond not to mention it to their friend.

3. Rosamond thinks Ladislaw knows of the codicil and has stayed because he and Dorothea are so in love that they will marry. She is also bored and wants to stir him up.

4. Trumbull invites Ladislaw to an auction in order to bid on some paintings. Raffles manages to be there at the same time.

5. Raffles questions Ladislaw about his mother's name, whether his father had been ill, and if his parents still live.

6. Raffles has used up most of the 200 pounds Bulstrode gave him to go away and be quiet; now he wants more money.

7. Bulstrode is afraid Raffles will tell Ladislaw the truth. Bulstrode decides to offer Ladislaw a financial settlement.

8. Ladislaw thinks Bulstrode's proposal is thoroughly dishonorable. The money was earned by thievery and the employment of convicts.

9. Ladislaw wants to see Dorothea one last time to tell her that he is still going to London to earn his living at writing and speaking. He has decided to never come back to Middlemarch.

10. Dorothea and he meet accidentally in her uncle's library. She goes there to flee Mrs. Cadwallader. He is there looking for some papers.

Suggested Essay Topics

1. Why do you agree or disagree with Ladislaw that it would be dishonorable to share in the profits earned by thievery?

2. Using specific references from the text, explain why Rosamond is so disillusioned with her life.

SECTION EIGHT

Book Seven:
Two Temptations

Chapters 63–67

New Characters:

Toller, Minchen, Chichely: *Middlemarchers who are opposed to Lydgate's medical practices and position in the new hospital*

Standish: *lawyer who wrote Featherstone's first wills*

Summary

Toller, Minchen, and Chichely visit with Farebrother. They discuss Lydgate and his expenses. Farebrother suspects he may be taking opiates. At a New Year's Day party, Farebrother notices Vincy speaks as little as possible to his son-in-law. Rosamond seems to disregard her husband. Farebrother finds a moment to discreetly offer Lydgate help, which only causes Lydgate to privately consider suicide. He now needs 1,000 pounds to settle his debts. He continues to curtail their expenditures, further alienating Rosamond. She attempts to dictate how he practices in order to raise more capital; this enrages him. He explains that Ned Plymdale will be marrying soon and would be interested in their house and furnishings. She cries, having thought the security on the inventory of the furniture was actual payment of the debts. She accuses her husband of liking the curtailment of their spending and blames him for their predicament.

She goes to see Ned's mother the next day, then Trumbull, to cancel Lydgate's order to sell their house. That evening she tells her husband that Ned has taken a different house. She doesn't say she has seen Trumbull. She wheedles the size of the debt from Lydgate and, without his knowledge, writes to his uncle the next day. They argue bitterly when she tells Lydgate of her visit to Trumbull. She accuses him of misrepresenting himself before their marriage. She wants to leave Middlemarch rather than move to a small house on Bride Street.

Three weeks into the new year, a reply comes from Sir Lydgate. He castigates Lydgate for hiding behind his wife and refuses the request for the loan. A furious and frustrated Lydgate tells his wife he had considered going to Quallingham himself but rejected the idea as unworthy. Now she has gone behind his back. Lydgate begs for confidence and openness between them. She turns this back on him, saying he does not appreciate her efforts to make their marriage more pleasant. She demands an apology. Once again, he tries to make amends.

Desperate for money and under the influence of opiates, he takes to gambling at billiards. Fred finds him and quickly thinks of a way to get him to leave. Before he can implement his plan, Farebrother arrives and asks Fred to meet him. Fred interrupts Lydgate, asking him if he'd like to see Farebrother, too. When Lydgate defers, Fred lies and tells his brother-in-law that he is afraid to see Farebrother alone. The three leave together; Farebrother and Fred walking together, Lydgate going his own way.

Farebrother warns Fred that Mary may find another if Fred goes back to his old ways. Farebrother says he is still interested in Mary. Fred protests his innocence and makes it clear he will do nothing to lose Mary's love. Farebrother reassures him Mary loves Fred.

After losing at billiards, Lydgate feels he must apply to Bulstrode for a loan. He is so against taking this action that he fantasizes about leaving Middlemarch as Rosamond wants. He decides that is not feasible. After much procrastination, he speaks to Bulstrode. Bulstrode tells Lydgate he is leaving Middlemarch and taking time off from his business affairs, including the new hospital. He will no longer be contributing to the hospital, and suggests it combine with the Infirmary (the old hospital). Dorothea could be appealed to for more funds. Bulstrode has asked Dorothea to take his place as director. She has gone away and will give a decision when she returns. He obliquely denies Lydgate's request for a loan.

Analysis

Lydgate's situation is becoming untenable. At one time, he privately contemplates suicide; although he quickly dismisses this idea, he is taking opiates in an attempt to ameliorate his dark feelings about his life. His father-in-law, having been approached by Rosamond (without Lydgate's knowledge) for a loan, practically ignores him. Rosamond disregards his wishes, having gone to her father and Sir Lydgate for money. She has also defied her husband by telling Trumbull to take their house and furniture off the market. She feels he has worsened, not bettered, her situation and made false promises before they were married. Bulstrode is going, taking his financial support and his championing of Lydgate with him, leaving Lydgate to seek Dorothea's money for the hospital and the new idea of combining the old and new hospitals. Even his drugged attempt to earn money by gambling at the Green Dragon is a failure. Bulstrode rejects Lydgate's request for a loan. Farebrother had offered financial assistance, which Lydgate's pride would not allow him to accept. Lydgate becomes bitter. He is in debt, has an unsupportive, spoiled, selfish wife, no apparent solution to his problems, and his dream of running the new hospital according to the medical practices he has brought from France is effectively dashed. There is a desperation in him now. He is not the same ambitious, eager young doctor who arrived in Middlemarch not that long ago and promptly fell in love with a lovely, albeit superficial, woman.

Lydgate's financial situation may be symbolic of England's economic depression, which began in 1816 after the French Revolution. Taxes had already been raised fivefold and were kept at five percent higher than the prewar taxes, although they were lowered from the wartime ten percent. Currency was inflated by issuing pound notes, which were not convertible to gold. A bad harvest, the massive discharge of soldiers, the drastic fall of agricultural prices, rents, and profits all were partially responsible. This was less than a decade and a half before the novel takes place.

Study Questions

1. What do the Middlemarch locals have to say about Lydgate on New Year's Day?

2. Of what does Farebrother speak privately to Lydgate?

3. What is Lydgate's plan as a partial solution to his money woes?

4. In what way does Rosamond thwart her husband's plan?

5. For what reason has his uncle sent Lydgate a nasty letter?

6. What is the purpose of Fred's being at the Green Dragon?

7. To convince Lydgate to leave the Green Dragon, Fred uses what lie?

8. What is the content of Farebrother's discussion with Fred?

9. Lydgate receives what news from Bulstrode?

10. After their latest argument about finances, for what does Lydgate implore Rosamond?

Answers

1. The locals are discussing Lydgate's debt, his medical practice, his marriage, and the new hospital. The locals seem severely disapproving of Lydgate.

2. Lydgate is discreetly drawn aside and offered a loan by Farebrother, who is well aware of Lydgate's spending habits and financial condition.

3. Lydgate plans to have Trumbull sell his house and furniture to Ned Plymdale, who is marrying and will have need of these. This will not solve his problem, but by moving to a smaller house on Bride Street, the Lydgates will have less outlay each month.

4. Rosamond visits Ned's mother and neglects to mention their house. Mrs. Plymdale says the young couple has found a possibility but are still looking. Rosamond then goes to Trumbull and orders him to take their house off the market.

5. Without her husband's knowledge, Rosamond has written to his uncle requesting a loan. Sir Lydgate, thinking Lydgate asked Rosamond to write the letter on his behalf, severely chides Lydgate for hiding behind his wife when asking for a loan and refuses.

6. Since Mary is otherwise occupied this particular evening, he decides to treat himself to a night out at the Green Dragon, not to gamble, just to play.

7. Fred was going to say Rosamond needed Lydgate. Before he had the chance, Farebrother sent a message to the billiard room that he was downstairs and wanted to see Fred. Fred sees this as an opportunity to trick Lydgate into leaving by saying he was afraid Farebrother was going to scold him for being in the Green Dragon.

8. After quickly saying good night to Lydgate, Farebrother does indeed scold Fred. He reminds Fred that he mustn't do anything to lose Mary's faith in him and cause her to seek another. Farebrother also assures Fred he will not seek Mary, although he cares for her, since he knows Mary does love Fred.

9. Bulstrode tells Lydgate that he is leaving his home, his business affairs, and the new hospital.

10. Lydgate feels the alienation and distance between his wife and him and blames it on, among other matters, her acting without discussing issues with him first. He implores her to share confidences with him as well as to be open with him. He thinks trust is necessary in their marriage.

Suggested Essay Topics

1. Rosamond's and Lydgate's marriage has rapidly deteriorated. Plot the events that led to this condition.

2. Farebrother is both Fred's and Mary's friend and is in love with Mary. Using examples from the text, explain how it is possible for him to be both.

Chapters 68–71

New Characters:

Mrs. Abel: *Bulstrode's servant at Stone Court who nurses the ill Raffles while Bulstrode sleeps*

Hawley: *a Middlemarch lawyer who inquires into the rumors about Bulstrode's conduct with Raffles*

Hopkins: *the undertaker who buried Raffles*

Summary

Raffles visited Bulstrode. Bulstrode was terrified his wife would overhear Raffles' ranting and raving. He offered Raffles the choice between having money for the rest of his life in return for his silence and disappearance from Middlemarch or having a policeman remove him. If he should tell his tales, Bulstrode swears no one will believe them. Raffles left a richer, sicker man.

As Bulstrode prepares for his delayed departure from Middlemarch, he asks Caleb to recommend a manager for Stone Court. Caleb decides Fred would be the man for this, under Caleb's supervision. He wants to ask Bulstrode if Fred may also live there while managing the estate. Bulstrode is resistant, but his wife—who is Vincy's sister—intercedes for her nephew. Bulstrode agrees. Caleb takes his wife's advice, and says nothing of this to Fred for the time being. Caleb goes to the bank to see Bulstrode, in order to inform him there is a sick man at Stone Court named Raffles. Lydgate must be called. Raffles has also told Caleb of Bulstrode's background, which causes Caleb to resign from the management of Stone Court. Fred will not have his opportunity. Bulstrode has difficulty accepting Caleb's resignation. It means he believes Raffles. When it is clear Caleb is passing no judgment, he asks Caleb not to repeat Raffles' charges to anyone. Caleb is indignant but agrees.

Bulstrode rushes to Stone Court, hoping to get there before Lydgate, and is shocked at how much sicker Raffles is. He is clearly out of his mind. Lydgate arrives and diagnoses the case as dangerous only if mismanaged; he instructs Bulstrode to have his servants keep Raffles away from liquor. Bulstrode insists he will stay and

see to this himself. Lydgate arrives home to find the agent of one of his creditors and Rosamond hiding in her bedroom. The next morning, she goes to her father's, only to return saying her parents want her to stay with them for a while. She sees he does not want her to go.

Bulstrode searches Raffles' pockets for evidence of where he might have been spreading Bulstrode's past. The delirious Raffles refuses the food Lydgate has ordered for him. When Lydgate arrives, he sees that Raffles is worse and prescribes moderate amounts of opium to induce sleep, repeating that the amount must not be surpassed and liquor must be kept from the man. Bulstrode explains he has sent word to his wife and will stay with Raffles himself. Bulstrode gives Lydgate the 1,000 pound loan, saying his wife wanted to help her niece. Bulstrode had been too hasty in refusing the loan.

Bulstrode, exhausted from sitting up with Raffles, must sleep. He asks Mrs. Abel to administer the opium and explains the dosage. He debates sending for Lydgate. He realizes he forgot to tell Mrs. Abel when to stop giving Raffles the opium. He decides not to. Mrs. Abel begs Bulstrode to give Raffles some brandy to ease his struggle with his illness. Bulstrode gives her the key to the wine-cooler. Later, Mrs. Abel tells him Raffles seems to be in a coma. Bulstrode goes to check, taking the opium phial and brandy bottle away with him. Lydgate arrives to find Bulstrode sitting with a dying man.

Lydgate is once again approached by Farebrother, who has heard of the creditor invading Lydgate's home. Lydgate tells him he has headed off his creditors. Farebrother asks if Lydgate has incurred a new debt to pay off the old. Lydgate tells him of Bulstrode's loan.

The locals at the Green Dragon gossip about Bulstrode's past, Raffles' appearance, Caleb's resignation from Bulstrode's employ, Ladislaw's genealogy, and Lydgate's treating Raffle. Later, the inference is drawn that Lydgate's debts being paid have a lot to do with Raffles' death and Bulstrode's "loan" to Lydgate. At a meeting in Town Hall, when Lydgate and Bulstrode walk in together, glances pass between the other Middlemarchers. Hawley demands Bulstrode's resignation from public position, or the denial of the allegations the now deceased Raffles has made. After protesting, a stricken Bulstrode rises to leave but stumbles. Lydgate goes to his aid and walks him out. He is beginning to suspect the loan was a bribe. After the meeting, Farebrother and Brooke go to Dorothea's. They tell her all. She decides they must find out the truth and clear Lydgate.

Analysis

Ugly rumors and half-truths are neither confirmed nor denied. Bulstrode has managed to drag Lydgate's reputation down with his own by allowing Mrs. Abel to unwittingly kill Raffles. Lydgate appears to have accepted a bribe to murder Raffles. Lydgate is beginning to doubt the loan, wondering if it is a bribe for not revealing that Raffles' death was not accidental nor natural. Farebrother asks if Lydgate had taken a loan to cover his debts not knowing that Lydgate may be implicated in murder. The locals, with the lawyer Hawley at their helm, waste no time in piecing together the information they have. If only they had not gone beyond the facts, Lydgate would not be aligned with Bulstrode. This is the logical assumption. Bulstrode brought Lydgate to Middlemarch to be the chief medical superintendent of the new hospital in the first place. Lydgate has married Bulstrode's niece. Hawley realizes there is no legal foundation for accusing Bulstrode, but he wants the truth and demands it in the town meeting. Bulstrode deftly avoids answering by accusing the others of chicanery. No issues are laid to rest. Only Dorothea runs to clear Lydgate's name.

This jumping to conclusions also had its place in the recent history of Marian Evans' England. Lord Grey, the Prime Minister at the time of the passage of the Reform Act, was considered a champion of the people. He, however, was not so greatly in favor of the bill. He was, at his own admission, a conservative who only wanted to prevent the revolution threatened if the bill failed to pass.

Study Questions

1. Why has Raffles returned to Stone Court?
2. For what reason does Caleb decline to work for Bulstrode?
3. Lydgate has left what instructions concerning Raffles?

4. In what manner does Bulstrode fulfill these instructions?

5. What has Mrs. Abel to do with Raffles' death?

6. What motive does Bulstrode have in changing his mind about the loan to Lydgate?

7. Farebrother has what purpose in stopping Lydgate to speak with him privately?

8. What is Hawley's logic in piecing together what he thinks has happened?

9. What happens to Bulstrode at the town meeting?

10. How is Lydgate further implicated in Bulstrode's guilt during the meeting?

Answers

1. Raffles is very ill and needs more money. Bulstrode offers him money for the rest of his life if he is silent and disappears. The only other option is no more money from Bulstrode and the chance of being called a liar when Raffles attempts to besmirch Bulstrode's reputation by telling what he knows.

2. Caleb picked up the ill Raffles on the road and brought him to Stone Court at Raffles' request. During the ride, Raffles told Caleb about Bulstrode's past.

3. Lydgate instructs Bulstrode to keep liquor from Raffles and offer him only the specified foods. When he returns and sees that Raffles' condition has taken a turn for the worse, he gives Bulstrode opium for Raffles, insisting that he administer small doses and only for a limited time. He repeats that Raffles must have no liquor.

4. Bulstrode personally follows Lydgate's instructions until he must sleep. Then he repeats them to Mrs. Abel, neglecting to mention that the opium may only be administered for a limited time. He realizes his mistake during the night, but does not rectify it.

5. Mrs. Abel has effectively and innocently murdered Raffles

by giving him too much opium and then, contrary to the directions given to Bulstrode, allowing the suffering man some brandy.

6. Bulstrode is fearful Lydgate will realize he has allowed Raffles to die. He gives the loan to Lydgate in an effort to help him fail to come to this realization. He says his wife convinced Bulstrode that he must help his niece, Lydgate's wife.

7. Farebrother has heard that the creditors were at Lydgate's. He is willing to offer his help once again. When Lydgate tells him he already has gotten the money to keep his house and furniture, Farebrother wonders if Lydgate has taken another loan.

8. Hawley encounters Bambridge, who tells him the story in the presence of Hopkins, who says he just buried Raffles the previous day. Bambridge mentions that Lydgate attended Raffles. He also confers with Wrench and Toller to validate Lydgate's diagnosis of Raffles' illness.

9. At the town meeting, Bulstrode is ordered to either resign from his public positions or deny the rumors concerning his past.

10. Before the meeting, Bulstrode and Lydgate accidentally arrive at the same time and walk in together. After being accused, Bulstrode is physically weakened, which only Lydgate is in a position to see. Lydgate escorts him out and has him taken home to bed. This appears to be the action of a dear friend and cohort.

Suggested Essay Topics

1. It is said that appearances are not always as they seem. Explain how this is true for Lydgate and Bulstrode.

2. Mrs. Abel has committed murder, but Bulstrode is the murderer. Explain how this theory may be proven using the text as your evidence.

SECTION NINE

Book Eight: Sunset and Sunrise

Chapters 72–80

New Character:

Martha: *the Lydgates' maid*

Summary

At the Chettams' dinner, Dorothea convinces Farebrother and Chettam that they must help her clear Lydgate's name. Celia implores her to listen to Chettam's advice. Lydgate must act for himself. Once having deposited Bulstrode at his home and reassuring Mrs. Bulstrode, Lydgate decides not to tell Rosamond, thinking the matter will soon become evident. The wives in the town discuss not only Bulstrode and Lydgate, but their spouses and not to the benefit of any of them. Mrs. Bulstrode, suspecting her husband's illness is not physical, seeks Lydgate, who gives her no satisfaction. Still seeking answers, Mrs. Bulstrode calls on the wives, one by one, and still gains no satisfaction. Finally, she calls upon her brother, who tells her everything. She locks herself in her room until that night. She tells her husband she knows and they cry together.

Rosamond, still hoping that Lydgate will move to London, is excited that Ladislaw has written to say he is coming to visit. Knowing nothing of her husband's latest trouble and not telling him what she is doing, she has invited guests to a party for Ladislaw. The

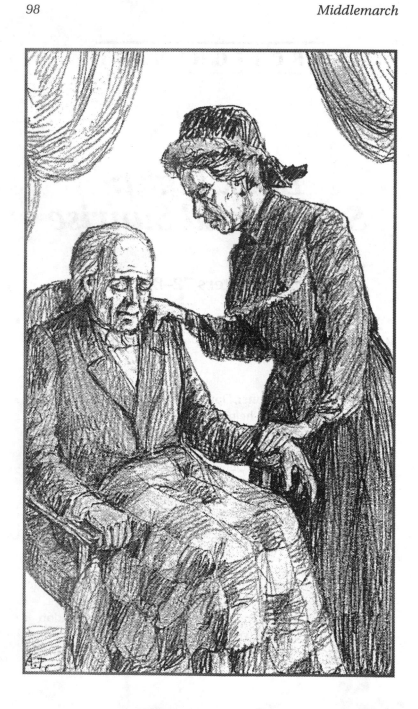

invitations are refused. When Lydgate sees one of them, he leaves
rather than vent his wrath on Rosamond. Rosamond goes to her
parents. Her father tells her all, protecting Lydgate in the telling.
Lydgate finally asks Rosamond what is troubling her. She confesses
she knows all. Each wallows in misery, thinking the other should
realize how hurtful this is. Once again, Rosamond says they must
move to London.

Dorothea calls Lydgate to her home to speak about the hospital and is shocked at the change in his appearance in such a short
time. She asks his opinion about the plans to proceed with what
Bulstrode originally laid out. He tells her she should not seek his
opinion. He may be leaving soon. She asks him straightforwardly
if that is because no one believes in him. She asks him to tell her
what happened. She promises she will not repeat what he says.
There are people in Middlemarch who believe in his innocence.
He complies. She convinces him to stay and direct the medical part
of the new hospital, as they had decided, with her supplying the
money. He is delighted but wants to consult Rosamond first, since
he thinks she will not want to stay. Dorothea asks if she may call
on Rosamond to convince her that staying is best. He decides he
cannot allow Dorothea to tell his wife of what has transpired. He
must leave Middlemarch. Dorothea succeeds in getting him to see
that he must not give up so easily. She would be honored to call
upon Rosamond. Before she does, she writes a check for 1,000
pounds to bring with her to give Lydgate to pay the debt to
Bulstrode.

Dorothea goes to visit Lydgate's wife full of hope, good news
and the desire to become friends with her. Seeing Ladislaw and
Rosamond alone in Lydgate's house, she leaves the envelope with
the check and flees to Freshitt Hall. Ladislaw is aghast that
Dorothea has found them alone together and has not stayed to
socialize. Rosamond is finally made to see that it is Dorothea, not
she, with whom he is in love. He leaves, the maid never having seen
him, wishing he could make amends with Rosamond. She faints
and remains out until her husband arrives home. Ladislaw returns
that evening, surprised that Rosamond has not told her husband
that he had been there and would return. The men commiserate
and Ladislaw takes his leave. Dorothea goes to the Farebrothers'

but is exhausted and leaves early. She stays up all night thinking and resolves to attempt a visit with Rosamond again the next day.

Analysis

The outcome of all the half-truths, mistaken meanings, thoughts unuttered, and feelings denied is close at hand. Rosamond learns that, despite her fantasizing and romanticizing, Ladislaw is not in love with her nor has he been. Dorothea, somehow finding strength within herself for a second attempt, will visit Rosamond the next day to explain Lydgate's situation. Her check will break the last connection Lydgate has with Bulstrode—the loan which is thought to be a bribe for either murdering Raffles or saying nothing of the knowledge of the murder of Raffles. Ladislaw speaks clearly to Rosamond; this not only allows her to understand that he is not in love with her, but it demonstrates he loves Dorothea and has all along, her marriage and the codicil to her husband's will notwithstanding. Lydgate has the opportunity to speak privately with Ladislaw. Although he does not delve into his feelings, he gives him the facts as he sees them and warns Ladislaw that he is involved. Bulstrode is his not-so-secret-anymore-step-grandfather.

Bulstrode and Mrs. Bulstrode have no secrets between them since Vincy told his sister all and she told her husband she knows. But Ladislaw still doesn't know Dorothea loves him.

This time, provinciality has its benefits. Dorothea will help her neighbors, asked or not. While both Ladislaw and Lydgate are new to Middlemarch, each is her neighbor, as is Rosamond. There is no more thought in her mind to allow Lydgate to "hang" without help as there was to separate from the husband she no longer loved. Rosamond, also reared provincially, is not at all surprised that Dorothea wants to help Lydgate nor that she has enlisted his other friends to help. The only one who seems to be somehow surprised is Ladislaw. He is very much concerned with his own misery.

Study Questions

1. What is foremost in Dorothea's mind when she hears of Lydgate's troubles?

2. In sending for Lydgate, what is Dorothea's supposed purpose?

3. Why hasn't Lydgate told Rosamond of his troubles yet?

4. What has happened to Bulstrode?

5. How is Rosamond made even more distraught?

6. In what manner has it happened that the Lydgates' maid doesn't know Ladislaw is at their home?

7. What does Dorothea bring with her to the Lydgates' home?

8. Why doesn't Dorothea stay to speak with Rosamond as she had promised?

9. When Dorothea arrives at the Farebrothers', what happens?

10. How is it that Rosamond and Lydgate still have not discussed the latest troubles he has, even though Rosamond knows of them through her father?

Answers

1. Dorothea is determined that Lydgate's friends must act to clear his name despite Chettam's insistence that a man must act to clear his own name.

2. Dorothea sends for Lydgate, supposedly to determine strategy for keeping the new hospital separate from the old one.

3. Lydgate is so angry with and feels so distant from his wife that he simply decides to let her hear of his latest troubles. He hopes the news reaches her through someone else. He doesn't want to face her selfishness and coldness while telling her himself.

4. Bulstrode has been ill since the town meeting. His wife suspects it is not physical and keeps looking for answers, finally finding some from her brother.

5. Rosamond has filled her emptiness with romantic fantasies about a relationship with Ladislaw instead of directing her energies toward Lydgate. When Dorothea sees Ladislaw and Rosamond alone and retreats in obvious distress, Ladislaw tells Rosamond the truth.

6. The maid, Martha, did not see Ladislaw arrive and thinks Rosamond is still walking in the garden when Dorothea arrives. She goes to search for Rosamond while Dorothea enters the drawing room to wait. When Martha opens the drawing-room door for Dorothea, Martha neither enters nor looks in the room.

7. Dorothea brings a check for 1,000 pounds to the Lydgates so that they may repay Bulstrode and sever the last remaining connection to him.

8. Dorothea is so distressed at finding Ladislaw alone with Rosamond that she politely flees, rather than staying to speak to her as she had promised Lydgate.

9. The kitten has taken the tortoiseshell lozenge-box Ladislaw gave to Miss Noble. She looks under the chairs for it. Upon hearing it is a gift from Ladislaw, Farebrother joins his aunt in looking until it is found, explaining she is very attached to Ladislaw.

10. Rosamond has still not approached her husband about the latest troubles, thinking he should come to her first. He, in his turn, has not come to tell her because he fears her distance and coldness.

Suggested Essay Topics

1. Dorothea is the one who leads Lydgate's friends to clear his name. Validating your opinion with examples from the text, why do you think it was she, rather than another friend, who insisted?

2. Bulstrode is no friend to Lydgate, yet when Bulstrode is overcome by his emotions, it is Lydgate who tends to him. Why does Lydgate act so kindly toward a man who has severely damaged whatever was left of his reputation?

Chapters 81–86 and Finale

Summary

When Dorothea reaches the Lydgates' home, Dr. Lydgate is still there and tells her he is certain his wife will see her. First, he wants to thank Dorothea for the check. Afraid of having to tell her husband why she declines to see Dorothea, Rosamond joins her in the drawing room, where she sees Dorothea is worn and close to tears. The two women talk and cry together as Dorothea gently explains how the problem was not Lydgate's fault. He did not tell Rosamond for fear of hurting her even more. Dorothea allows Rosamond to see her pain, which serves to begin a friendship between them. Rosamond confesses to Dorothea that she received the wrong impression the day before; Ladislaw was really telling Rosamond he was in love with another. Later, Lydgate and Rosamond renew the warmth in their marriage.

Ladislaw returned to Middlemarch thinking to ask Bulstrode to finance an endeavor for him, but the thought of having any relations with his step-grandfather was awful to him. He still has not admitted to himself that the true purpose of this visit is solely to catch a glimpse of Dorothea. The night of Dorothea's second visit to Rosamond, Ladislaw visits and is received coldly by Rosamond, who secretly gives him a note saying she has told Dorothea all. Two days later, Miss Noble brings Ladislaw to Lowick Manor, asking Dorothea to see him. They are soon in each others' arms, with Dorothea telling Ladislaw of her private fortune.

Brooke joins the Chettams and Cadwalladers in order to tell them of the impending marriage, just three weeks hence. Chettam is angry and blames Brooke that Dorothea will lose her inheritance from Casaubon. Celia goes to Lowick Manor to try to talk some sense into her sister only to learn that she is, indeed, marrying Ladislaw and that they will be living in London. Bulstrode lives in fear of never making amends with his wife and offers to gladly comply when she asks him to aid her niece. However, he explains, he cannot. Lydgate has written him rejecting any services from Bulstrode ever again. Bulstrode suggests they help Fred instead by placing him at Stone Court. He confides that Caleb will have no dealings with Bulstrode and Mrs. Bulstrode must see Caleb herself. Caleb tells Mary, who in turn tells Fred, who at first thinks she is jesting.

Fred and Mary lead an exemplary (although not rich) life, each doing some writing, in addition to raising their three sons. Lydgate died at 50, thinking himself a failure, despite his having a good income, a charming wife, and four children. Ladislaw goes into Parliament. Dorothea raises the children, these children being the reason Chettam forgot his anger with her. Brooke lived to the proverbial "ripe old age."

Analysis

Through Rosamond's intervention, Ladislaw is made to understand Dorothea knows he does not love Rosamond. With Miss Noble's help, he goes to see Dorothea himself. They do marry and he becomes a member of Parliament, probably incorporating her plans with his own thoughts, while she remains home with their children. With Dorothea's intervention, Lydgate and Rosamond resume a loving marriage, enriched by children and ending with his death at the age of 50. Brooke lives to be a much older man and leaves his property to his great-nephew, who could have stood for Parliament, but, unlike his great uncle, chooses not to. Celia and Chettam are reconciled when Dorothea's first child is born. Chettam cannot bear to see his wife unhappy by his order to not see her sister. Fred and Mary marry and have sons. With Bulstrode's plans and Mrs. Bulstrode's implementation they take over the management of Stone Court (with Caleb's supervision) as originally planned. Fred and Mary, too, seem to have a meeting of the minds. No one is quite sure which of them wrote *Cultivation of Green Crops and the Economy of Cattle-Feeding*, although it was supposedly produced by Fred, or *Stories of Great Men, Taken from Plutarch*, supposedly written by Mary. While all turned out for the best, the route to the end result seems far too circuitous. There was so little direct communication between the players.

It is interesting that Brooke, a dissenter, contemplated standing for Parliament as soon as it became a possibility for those not of the Anglican faith and when land ownership was no longer a requirement. His grand-nephew was not interested in being a member of Parliament. Could it be that once Parliament had been accessible to non-landed dissenters for more than a generation, membership in it was no longer sought? While his son chose not to become a member of Parliament, Ladislaw had—sometime between the changes in the requirements to become a member due to the passage of the Reform Act and the time when these changes were accepted as the norm.

Study Questions

1. For what reason does Rosamond see Dorothea?

2. What is Dorothea's method in convincing Rosamond that Lydgate is the injured party?

3. What does Dorothea have to say about the Lydgates' relationship?

4. During her meeting with Rosamond, why is Dorothea so sad?

5. In what way does Rosamond try to help Dorothea?

6. What is the purpose in Miss Noble's coming to Lowick Manor?

7. What information does Ladislaw give Dorothea?

8. What reaction did Chettam have to the news of Dorothea's impending marriage?

9. How is the reconciliation between the former Brooke sisters achieved?

10. How did Fred and Mary come to live at Stone Court?

Answers

1. Rosamond is afraid to refuse to see Dorothea. It is Lydgate who asks her to do so. She fears Dorothea may explain why she left the previous day.

2. Dorothea carefully explains that Lydgate's friends firmly believe he knew nothing of who Raffles was or what was done to him. He honestly believed Bulstrode thought he'd been too hasty in refusing the loan and changed his mind.

3. Dorothea reassures Rosamond that Lydgate had not explained this to her because it pained him too much to bring the matter up to her.

4. Dorothea is so sad because she thinks she is saving three lives, none of them her own. She still thinks Rosamond loves Ladislaw, and he her. She is trying to prevent Rosamond from decimating her marriage, destroying Lydgate, and damaging Ladislaw's honor by continuing this three-sided relationship. The worst sorrow for her is that she knows she loves Ladislaw, even though she still thinks he loves Rosamond.

5. That night, when Ladislaw is there, Rosamond slips him a note along with his teacup telling him she has told Dorothea that he doesn't love her, but Dorothea.

6. Ladislaw fears Dorothea will not see him so he asks Miss Noble, of whom they are both fond, to request that she see him.

7. Ladislaw tells Dorothea he's sorry he hadn't told her of his lineage himself. Bulstrode had offered him money in an attempt to make amends, which he refused. He knows he will be poor and feels he must leave. He would rather be with her.

8. Chettam had been angry to hear that Dorothea would be marrying Ladislaw and blamed Brooke for allowing her to throw away her inheritance from Casaubon like this.

9. When Dorothea gives birth to her first child, Celia cries to her husband that her sister will harm the baby by not knowing what to do. Chettam bows to his wife's tears and the sisters are reconciled.

10. Bulstrode wants very much to make amends with his wife. When she asks him to help Rosamond, he explains he can't. Lydgate has severed all relations with him. Then he suggests he help Fred by telling Mrs. Bulstrode to ask Caleb to allow Fred to manage Stone Court (under Caleb's supervision) and live there.

Suggested Essay Topics

1. Rosamond and Dorothea have achieved happy marriages through mutual help. How have they helped each other?

2. Bulstrode, who could have helped Fred in the very beginning of his troubles, ends up helping Fred when he is no longer a desperate young man. How has this turned out to be to Fred's benefit?

SECTION TEN

Sample Analytical Paper Topics

Topic #1

Four pairs of lovers have achieved successful marriages through very different, difficult paths. How did they do this?

Outline

I. Thesis Statement: *In George Eliot's* Middlemarch, *four couples have circuitously followed various paths to happy marriages.*

II. Dorothea and Ladislaw

    A. Ladislaw's repudiation of Casaubon's financial support

    B. Rosamond's admission to Dorothea that Ladislaw loves only Dorothea

    C. Ladislaw's return to Middlemarch to tell Dorothea he would not cause her to become penniless by marrying her regardless of the codicil to her deceased husband's will

    D. Dorothea's explaining that she has a private income other than her inheritance

III. Rosamond and Lydgate

    A. Dorothea's visiting Rosamond to proclaim Lydgate's innocence and dread of further hurting his wife

    B. Ladislaw's declaration of love for Dorothea, not her

    C. Bulstrode's leaving town and any association with Lydgate

    D. Dorothea's loan of 1,000 pounds so that they may not be in debt to Bulstrode and still keep their home

IV. Fred and Mary

    A. Fred finishing school

    B. Mary declaring her love for Fred, not Farebrother

    C. Caleb employing Fred

    D. Mrs. Bulstrode asking her husband to help her family which leads him to tell her to have Caleb engage Fred (under his supervision) to manage Stone Court and reside in it with Mary

V. Celia and Chettam

    A. Dorothea telling Celia she views Chettam as an excellent brother-in-law

    B. Chettam liking Dorothea's plans for the cottages and wanting to build them on his estates

    C. Dorothea marrying Casaubon and leaving for a six-week honeymoon

    D. Chettam continuing to come to Tipton Grange to discuss the cottages and staying to chat with Celia

Topic #2

Ladislaw is something of a mystery until well into the novel. How has George Eliot constructed his secrets to keep him a mystery?

Outline

I. Thesis Statement: *Ladislaw's background makes him one of the most mysterious characters in the novel.*

II. Connection with Casaubon

    A. Ladislaw's grandmother and Casaubon's mother were sisters

    B. Dorothea sees a portrait of Ladislaw's grandmother and is told by Casaubon that she made an "unfortunate" marriage

    C. Casaubon had been supporting both Ladislaw's mother (until her death) and Ladislaw (until he returns from Rome)

III. Connection with Bulstrode

    A. Bulstrode's first wife was Ladislaw's grandmother

    B. Ladislaw's mother had run away to the stage before her own mother married Bulstrode

    C. Bulstrode denied Ladislaw's mother her share of her father's (the deceased husband of Bulstrode's first wife) business

    D. Raffles recognizes Ladislaw's name when visiting Bulstrode

    E. Bulstrode offers Ladislaw his mother's share of the business

IV. Childhood

    A. Ladislaw knew nothing of his grandparents' business, his grandfather's demise, or his grandmother's remarriage

    B. Ladislaw's father died young of a disease which emaciated him

    C. Ladislaw's mother had to apply to Casaubon for the money they needed to live

    D. Casaubon supported them only financially, having no other interest in either Ladislaw or his mother

V. Recently

    A. Visits his second cousin, Casaubon, at Lowick Manor

    B. Studies art in Rome under his friend, Naumann

    C. Returns to Middlemarch where he is the editor of *Pioneer* for Brooke

    D. Is greatly disliked by Casaubon who is jealous

Topic #3

Sometimes, young people need a mentor—someone other than a parent or relative—during their young adulthood. How has Farebrother filled this role for both Fred and Lydgate?

Outline

I.   Thesis Statement: *Farebrother plays the role of mentor to both Fred and Lydgate.*

II.   Fred

    A.   Advises him to finish school

    B.   Acts as his emissary to the Garths when his shame at being unable to repay the loan Caleb co-signs prevents him from going

    C.   Speaks to Mary on Fred's behalf to see if she still will not marry him if he becomes a clergyman now that he has finished school

    D.   Calls Fred downstairs in the Green Dragon reminding him not to do anything to make him unworthy of Mary's love

III.   Lydgate

    A.   Befriends him when he is new to Middlemarch and urges him to distance himself from Bulstrode and stay out of debt

    B.   Notices when Lydgate starts taking opium and asks if he can help

    C.   When he hears of the inventory people coming to Lydgate's house, once again offers his help

    D.   Is pleased when Lydgate tells him he has the money but asks if he borrowed again to stay the inventory

IV.   Denies Self to Help his Young Friends

    A.   Is in love with Mary, but speaks to her on Fred's behalf

    B.   Tells Lydgate that Bulstrode will call him an enemy if he doesn't vote as Bulstrode directed, but that he (Farebrother) will like him just the same even if Lydgate votes for his opponent

C. Rather than gamble at the Green Dragon, calls Fred down to remind him not to gamble

D. Offers an uneven trade of equipment which would benefit Lydgate

Bibliography

Allen, Walter. *George Eliot.* New York: Macmillan Publishing Co., 1964.

Arnstein, Walter L. *Britain Yesterday and Today: 1830 to Present,* 6th edition. Massachusetts: D.C. Heath & Co., 1992.

Ashton, Rosemary, ed. *Penguin Classics: George Eliot—Middlemarch.* New York: Penguin Group, 1994.

Bloom, Harold, ed. *Critical Interpretations: George Eliot's Middlemarch.* New York: Chelsea House Publishers, 1987.

Draper, James P., ed. *World Literature Criticism: 1500 to the Present, Vol. 2.* Michigan: Gale Research, Inc., 1992.

Haight, Gordon S., ed. *The George Eliot Letters.* Connecticut: Yale University Press, 1954-55.

Hornback, Bert G., ed. *A Norton Critical Edition: Middlemarch.* New York: W. W. Norton & Co., 1977.

McHenry, Robert, ed. in chief. *The New Encyclopedia Britannica,* Vol. 4. Illinois: University of Chicago Press, 1993.

Roberts, Clayton and David Roberts. *A History of England, Vol. 2,* 2nd edition. New Jersey: Prentice-Hall, Inc., 1985.

Showalter, Elaine. *A Literature of Their Own: British Women Novelists from Brontë to Lessing.* New Jersey: Princeton University Press, 1977.

Speck, W. A., *A Concise History of Britain 1707–1975.* New York: Cambridge University Press, 1993.

Taylor, Ina. *The Life of George Eliot: A Woman of Contradictions.* New York: William Morris and Co., Inc., 1989.